Moneylove 3.0 Vol 3

New Digital Age Sequel

From

A Pioneering Prosperity Teacher

by

Jerry Gillies

Edited by Tony Busse

ALSO BY JERRY GILLIES

MONEYLOVE: How to Get the Money You Deserve for Whatever You Want

MEN ON WOMEN: 101 men Reveal Their deepest desires, Feelings and Fears

PSYCHOLOGICAL IMMORTALITY: Using Your Mind to Extend Your Life

TRANSCENDENTAL SEX: A Meditative Approach to Increasing Sexual Pleasure

FRIENDS: The Power and Potential of the Company You Keep

MY NEEDS, YOUR NEEDS, OUR NEEDS: A Handbooks For Discovering Each Other and Enhancing Your Love Potential

Editor's Note:

Moneylove 3.0 was originally published in digital format. It is so jammed packed with vital information and contains such a large amount of incredible content that each of the 12 Chapters could easily be books on their own. A print edition of this work would come in at over 700 pages - too cumbersome for many reasons! As a result we have elected to break it up into 3 Volumes that will each include the Introduction and several Chapters.

Welcome to the Third and Final Volume which will cover Chapters 10-12, the Instruction Manual for the Book, the Introduction and the Additional Resources Section.

His is a book unlike any you've read before and we strongly encourage you to follow Jerry's instructions on how to use the book and to heed his call to "Do the Damn Exercises!". It is our great hope that the ideas and exercises contained in these books will fill you with "Robust Expectations" and lead you to the "Joyful and Triumphant" results the author intended.

This book is dedicated to six good friends and mentors who would definitely have been a part of it if they were still around. Wait, they are still around in spirit and actually are a part of it.

Ray Bradbury

Leo Buscaglia

Norman Cousins

Ken Keyes, Jr.

Og Mandino

Ric Masten

Hip Hip Hooray!
My Acknowledgments

I know it's usual for an author to state he or she couldn't have written their book without the support and assistance of a sometimes long list of people. Not true in my case! I definitely could have written this without any help at all. Of course, it would have then been a very short and not nearly as good a book--but it could've been done.

One of the things I am most proud of in my life, and a way in which I have definitely left a major thumbprint on the world, is my excellent taste in choosing teachers and mentors and friends and colleagues. I have been so blessed with so many supporters and fantastic contributors to this work. Yes, Moneylove 3.0 might have still been written without the support of Rupa Cousins, Barry Dunlop, Christina Makrides, Leo Quinn, and Mary Ann Somervill--but not nearly as well or nearly as soon. My list of contributors, whom I also call faculty members, and whose wisdom added vast value and profound dimensions to this volume, I will list alphabetically:

Martin Boroson, Tony Busse, Marianne Cantwell, Rupa Cousins, Stephanie Donegan, Michael Dunlop, Barry Dunlop, David Friedman, Edwene Gaines, Allen Klein, Christina Makrides, Sonia Milton, Rickie Moore, Maria Nemeth, Joe Nuckols, Leo Quinn, SQuire Rushnell, Christine Segal, Nicholas Tart, Marta Vago, Maggy Whitehouse, Barbara Winter.

I did not include their titles and the many books they've written, since I elaborate on all of that in the segments or Books in which their contributions appear in the upcoming pages. Along with Internet links for most of them to find out more about them. To everyone involved in this transformative creation, my deeply felt gratitude and reverence. In one of the many ways Moneylove 3.0 is different than other books, when I look over that list, I see not only contributors, and distinguished collaborators, but new and old friends, and it is a heartwarming experience indeed to know how much they gave of themselves and their wisdom to make this a unique and highly conscious effort.

Volume 3: Books 10 through 12 of Moneylove 3.0

CONTENTS

Book Ten:Laughing All The Way 26

Inspired by a quote from Og Mandino, this book looks at how valuable humor can be, and how important having fun making money can be in creating total prosperity.

Chapter Eleven: QuoteLove 54

You may have thought you loved quotes and gained a lot of wisdom from them, but you ain't seen nothing yet! The introduction of Jerry's powerful new tool, Quotercises, designed to exponentially increase the impact your favorite quotes have on your life, momentum, and fulfillment. There's 100 of these little exercises, so this book can provide years of positive experiences just by itself.

Book Twelve: Weapons of Mass Distraction 86

Another exclusive Moneylove 3.0 creation, this final book contains seven of the most effective strategies for becoming happier, more prosperous, and a lot more fun.

Editor's Note: 97

Additional Resources: 98

Instruction Manual for Moneylove 3.0

"Everyone is flailing through this life without an owner's manual, with whatever modicum of grace and good humor we can manage."

Anne Lamott

Yes, you've got it right, this is your Instruction Manual for **Moneylove 3.0.** It's part of my quest to make this the most powerful learning tool it can be, as well as the most unique book ever produced. And I certainly don't want any readers flailing through it.

Of course, if you're like me, you'll immediately put it away and go right to the heart of the matter, starting with the Introduction. I cannot count the number of instruction manuals I have ignored. You'd think this ignoring would be the last thing, and least sensible thing I would do, considering how technologically-challenged I am. Even my high tech electric toothbrush and toaster give me problems from time to time. That's when I go to the instruction manual, and it's often too late then.

So maybe instead of an instruction manual, I should call this a learning aid, or an explanation of how to get more out of what I have written. No, I think I'll stick with Instruction Manual and leave you to your own devices in terms of how seriously you consider reading it or discarding it. **Moneylove 3.0** will definitely work amazingly well without it. But I can also safely say that those who put the time and energy in to read it and actually put some of the strategies I suggest into practice, will notice more immediate and more satisfying results.

And because I wouldn't ask you to do anything I wouldn't do--I just bought a high tech USB microphone (whatever that is) and I am going to read the instruction manual word for word.

A Sign of My Respect for You

I am <u>not</u> writing what I believe is a first, an Instruction Manual for a book, because I think you are so stupid you need one to get through it all.

This is not an act of condescension, but a way I have of demonstrating my appreciation and respect for you. I am assuming you are the kind of person who has always read my books, my blog, listened to my audios, or attended my workshops--a smart, self-aware, and self-appreciating human being on a positive path forward in his or her life.

My intention was really to give some guidelines to those who are capable of making it much <u>more</u> than a book. I think there is more in this manual to do with where you go with all this <u>information</u> and <u>knowledge</u> and <u>wisdom</u> (three separate and distinct things as I am sure you know) to turn it into a continuing training, teaching, and inspirational source in your life after your first read-through. While I also know you are more self-motivating than most people out there, I still wanted to provide you with some tools to put into action, because I know you are the kind of person who wants to get every last drop of usefulness out of this, much as the Eskimo uses every tiny part of the whale to improve his life.

The Big Secret

Well, I didn't know about it before, and am amazed to know some of my friends and colleagues didn't know about what you can do with a PDF file such as **Moneylove 3.0.** That is the fact that while, as most people do know, you cannot edit or delete parts of a PDF book, you <u>can</u> highlight any part of it, copy it, and then paste it into another document you create on your computer. Wow! When I recently discovered this, I saw how huge it can be when presenting a lot of ideas and concepts, and asking people to make these as personal and individual as possible to serve their needs and desires.

You can highlight and copy any passage that appeals to you, perhaps to focus on for one day, paste it onto a blank page in your word processing program, change the font or the size or even the color (or even print it out if you want to carry it around with you or paste it on your wall. For instance, I did the following with one of my favorite passages from Book Five, TimeLove:

Just changing your frame of reference, your

old **beliefs** and **habits** around time, can

dramatically and very quickly change your

life, your prosperity, and your energy and

feeling of self empowerment. The more

ways you discover to look at time, the more

flexible your thoughts will be on the subject.

We can highlight and paste a passage and turn some of the phrases contained within into our own affirmations. Again, from TIMELOVE:

We must realize that our experi-ence of time is what we

make of it, and the next step is to realize that we

actually create time. Then we realize that that we have

the power to enjoy the illusion of time, that time isn't

the enemy, and that we have the power to give time

creatively.

So what I did with this for myself:

I ACTUALLY CREATE TIME

TIME IS MY FRIEND

I HAVE THE POWER TO GIVE TIME CREATIVELY

And we can take a sentence we feel is powerful and important and play with it, helping to highlight it in our consciousness by creating it in different forms, colors, fonts, etc.

"I DECIDE HOw I wANT TO USE

MY TIME, AND wHAT
NEEDS TO GET DONE GETS DONE
wHEN I SAY IT GETS
DONE AND I CAN PAUSE AND
SMELL THE ROSES
wHENEVER I CHOOSE TO DO SO-
-I'M IN CHARGE."

Another Great Secret

This one I discovered quite by accident. I was taking a seven hour bus trip to Costa Rica from Panama City as I was editing **Moneylove 3.0.** I thought it would be great if I could get the unedited chapters onto my Kindle ebook reader. Well you can get WORD and PDF documents onto your Kindle, but the type is usually tiny, and there is no way to make the font larger. However, everyone with a Kindle has a personal email address. If you send the book or file you want to read on your Kindle from your computer to that address, and just put the word CONVERT in the subject line, Amazon will automatically, at no charge, send it to your Kindle in a form that will allow you to make the letters as large as you like just by going to Settings.

A Quite Different Book

One of the first things you will notice as you read **Moneylove 3.0** is that it is quite different from most books, perhaps all books, in several notable ways. For one thing, I have largely left unedited the comments from my contributors or interview subjects. I refuse to pander to short attention spans. Also, I felt it useful for you, as a reader, to get a sense of who was delivering these gems of wisdom and practical suggestions. I trust you are fully capable of finding them all, and you might even note the parts you find especially motivating, inspiring, or useful in a practical way. Too many so-called self-help books don't allow the reader to self-help at all, they strain and dilute and predigest the information like so much psychological or intellectual baby food. Also, if I did heavy editing, I might just cut out something someone said that would be very significant for you.

When Is a Book Not a Book?

It is not merely a conceit when I say **Moneylove 3.0** is much more than a book, and when I call individual sections of this volume, Books instead of Chapters. You see, every one of the following 12 sections are very much complete books on their own. And in fact, the Moneylove Team and I have discussed eventually releasing them as separate short books in Kindle versions. This is even true for the very short book that The Foreplay of Success is. I honestly believe that this first little book may be the most important piece of the whole prosperity puzzle. If you take the advice from what is now called Book One, and apply it, you will notice a dramatic shift in your ability to succeed on a focused and productive path.

A Select Library Rather Than a Big Book

So calling this entire collection of ideas, strategies, action exercises, and profound mini-seminars from my contributing faculty a book would be rather silly. (Though I promise not to laugh in the face of anyone who asks, "May I buy your book?") It is rather a complete library of the most cutting edge and effective ideas and tools ever created on the subject of total prosperity in every area of one's life. As a library, it is comparatively small with just 12 volumes inside, but these 12 Books can be borrowed anytime you want, for as long as you desire, and there is no penalty, in fact there is a huge reward, for keeping them!

Another way this is more a library or a collection of individual books is the fact that the 12 sections are in no particular order of importance. Unlike a book that starts in the beginning and follows an organic progression to the end, you can choose to start with any of the 12 books and stay with it until you accomplish some transformational results through the ideas contained within that trigger solutions from your own imagination. If you are now employed and want to be self-employed, by all means go right to Book Nine, titled **Jobs and No Jobs**. If you would like a life filled with more humor and fun, by all means choose to first read Book Ten, **Laughing All the Way**. Or, if you want to know more about being successful online, read Book Eight, **Cyber Consciousness** first.

Since the 12 Books herein are all focused on different aspects of prosperity and changing your life by changing something you are now doing (or something you are not doing enough of, or even something you are doing too much of), it makes sense to me that not everyone will consider the order I have put the 12 segments into suits them best. So put them in your own order of preference.

One final note on this. If you feel a lot more comfortable calling the individual sections of Moneylove 3.0 chapters instead of books, I will not be offended. As with everything in this volume, do what works for you.

A Clear Vision

I have a very clear vision of what i want to achieve and it's an ambitious one. I want you to immediately start using some of the suggestions to change every aspect of your life for the better. It's certainly not all about or just about money, though I would love to see you get rich. If you work at it and thus it works for you, then I cannot help but benefit. And I hope <u>you</u> have a clear vision of what you want to achieve.

I don't mean to insult you or myself, but we have not been keeping up. **Moneylove 3.0** is about how to become more prosperous in a rapidly changing economy and happier in a rapidly changing world. presenting timeless principles in a new way to help you succeed in one of the most transformational periods in human history. Almost nothing is as we knew it ten or twenty years ago, and it would be impossible for any human being to have kept up with all the changes. Things have been moving so rapidly in technology, science, the economy, global relationships, and even social interaction that few people have had the time to step back, go inward, and reflect on exactly what the hell is happening--to the world, their work, and the people they once knew and loved.

My Contributors are Actually a Prosperity Faculty

One of the biggest ways in which this is a unique creation is in that I invited some of the authors, teachers, coaches, and mentors I most admire and have learned from to make major contributions in sharing their own thoughts and ideas on my subject. You will notice that their segments are sometimes unusually long. That's because I wanted you to be able to get as much of their good stuff as possible. For most of them, I have included a live link, a way you can just click on their website for more of what they offer.

There is enough information in Moneylove 3.0 to get you moving in the right direction. Human growth, elevation, enlightenment, and getting on the right path with passion and purpose, is a lifelong process. It's also a process that can be fun, exciting, filled with promise and conscious results. But the best way to do it is one step at a time, and many gifted teachers and coaches suggest those be baby steps.

Here is one way to go with all this that I think will be very effective:

1. Read this entire volume. By all means, when you enjoy a passage by one of my contributors, take a look at their website.

2. **Do the exercises and processes as you go along.** In addition to interviewing her extensively on her amazing grasp of the world of the Internet, I have borrowed and repeat frequently, Marianne Cantwell's admonition from her book, How To Be A Free Range Human, where she says: Do the damn exercises!

3. **Read it aloud, taking your time.** This is a powerful way to increase the power of any book you read offering new ideas about anything. It accesses a part of your brain that may not be reached by mere silent reading. Though you are welcome to find the best way to put this into practice, I suggest reading Moneylove 3.0 all the way through first, then going back and reading one chapter/book at a time out loud. You can do this alone, but if you know someone, a friend or loved one, you think would appreciate a particular section, read it to them. You can even do this with distant friends via Skype or FaceTime. Or, you can record your reading it out loud and create your own audio book.

On to The Graduate School of Getting More Involved

And here are a few more suggestions I would call my graduate school program for those who have already finished reading all of **Moneylove 3.0**, and would like to make it more an individual experience.

1.   Go to a fairly long book, like **TimeLove,** and edit it and rewrite it so that it is more to your liking, and keeps the points you think are most important. This will help you absorb more of the important ideas it contains, as well as giving you the experience that you are in charge of the information you take in. Being able to copy and paste this PDF digital book makes that a lot easier.

2. Get a few of your friends or colleagues together and tell them several important ideas you've read and really like. You can

make this a discussion group, and see if they can see the same useful ideas you

3. Write a two-part essay on, "What is Right about **Money-love 3.0** and What Can Be Improved in Future Editions?" It would be highly unlikely that we exactly agree on every idea and point I've written or elicited from my contributors. The more you can make this your own creative venture, in terms of your individual desires and comfort level, the better it will work for you.

4. When you feel you have actually gotten desired results from putting at least one of my ideas into action, write and tell me about it. Obviously, I like getting emails of this sort, but it also will allow you to crystalize what value you received, and perhaps give you some thoughts on how to get even more for yourself from this work.

5. Each week for the next year, pick one sentence from one segment that will serve as your prosperity mantra for that week. It should be a sentence that speaks to you, that motivates or inspirits you. You can decide to post it on your wall, or add it to your computer's desktop, and to write it out or read it out loud as many times as you think will work best for you. But mostly, this is the sentence you will see as your mission statement for this particular week.

These exercises are not gimmicks, but rather ways you can make **Moneylove 3.0** a more dynamic and powerful tool in your psychological arsenal. Give any or all of them a chance, and you will be amazed at how much more profoundly you will begin seeing changes in your results.

The sum, combined total of everything offered on the following pages, contains ideas and revelations that may surprise or even shock you. I do not come from a position that I am richer or smarter than you. But I can pretty well declare that I've spent more time studying and learning this stuff than you have, and I have been unusually fortunate to attract teachers and mentors, some famous and some not, who have been the cream of the crop in terms of wisdom and coming up with practical solutions and inspiring ideas for living a life of true abundance and joy.

I've attempted to make this experience circular and permanent rather than linear and temporary. That is, I am laying down certain rules, principles, and ideas about prosperity that you can keep dipping into as you keep moving forward and upward in your life.

This is designed to be more simply functional than the way much information is presented today, zipping past our perceptions and cerebral cortexes faster than we can take it all in, and then disappearing as it's forced out by the next new shiny thing.

This approach reflects my assertion that one of the new skills we all need moving forward in this new millennium (and so much has been happening so fast we sometimes forget it is a new millennium), one of the primary skills we all need to develop and keep honing is that of discernment, that of creating an inner editor to let the useful stuff in and keep the information overwhelm at bay. The new process about doing that inner editing, I call **The Law of Subtraction**, is presented in Book Three. It is a practical way to deal with what I have termed Information

Asphyxiation.

I have talked a lot about this being unique in many different ways. One of those ways is that it is not meant to be at its most effective by the reader starting at page one and going through to the end, whether that takes days or weeks. For many people that would be a good idea, but if you are one of those readers, you should know that you are cheating yourself if that is it, if you just read it once cover to cover, and then put it aside.

This is an experience more than it is a book. The good thing about that is that it has no deadline, you don't have to return it to the library, you are not racing to prepare for a test. I'm sure as you looked over the table of contents, you saw some subjects that most interested you. This is not a volume for masochists, you don't have to punish yourself by reading stuff that isn't speaking to you right now just to get a few pages further along, you can go right to that section. So, again, if Time is your big issue, definitely read Book Five, **TimeLove** and its Appendix right away, before anything else (except perhaps this Instruction Manual and the Introduction--but even these are not mandatory).

One part of this volume, in particular, is not designed to be read all the way through all at once, and that is Book Eleven, **QuoteLove**. Even if you are overly ambitious, if you wanted to apply all 100 Quotercises to each of the 100 included quotes in turn, it could take months and miss the point of my approach to living. Take it nice and easy, don't stress or punish yourself. The section or Book is a resource, as many of the sections are, meant to be revisited time and again. It might be fun to take maybe five of the Quotercises and try them out. And if you find it a worthwhile and rewarding process, look forward to going back on a regular basis. This is a learning program, but you set your own schedule and your own choices. There's a lot here, and I don't want to regret including so much because some folks overdose and need medical care.

This all will work best for you if you begin it as an adventure, do the damn exercises, and have as much fun as you possibly can in the process.

Introduction

Is money your main objective in reading about prosperity consciousness? You might want to give that some additional thought.

In conversations with fellow prosperity thinkers and teachers, it has become evident that the concept of prosperity has dramatically broadened and expanded in the past twenty years. Perhaps we have come to realize the reality that money is just a part of it.

When college students were studied in the 1960s, 1970s, even into the 1990s, a majority said their main goal was to learn what they had to learn to make a lot of money out in the world. A much different answer emerges from the students in the 2000s. They want to find a career that excites their passion; they want to have a positive effect on the world; they want to keep learning and have fun, and money usually follows all these motivating factors. It is still important, but not as exclusively important as it once was.

And it isn't the top item offered when Silicon Valley companies, (or forward thinking companies in other parts of the world) are trying to hire bright young innovators. This is why so many of those companies have large recreational play areas on their campuses, and offer lots of interesting courses free to employees.

To put it another way, when a bunch of people were asked what their three wishes would be if a genie suddenly popped out of a lamp or bottle, very few of them listed money first, and some didn't even include it among the top three wishes. Health and a long and vital life were often picked, a happy life filled with lots of love was up there, being successful at

something they really loved doing and that made a difference in the world came up often. Here's the point, I believe:

If you are happy and fulfilled, money is not very important, though there is no doubt money can smooth the way on your path to happiness and fulfillment. A second part of the equation is that when you are happy and fulfilled, it is easier to create more money in your life. Other people are more attracted to you and want to buy whatever you are offering, be it a product, a service, or your valuable ideas.

Of course, money has a lot more significance in your life if you are worrying about the lack of it, or don't believe you deserve it or don't feel capable of producing it.

Though this book is based on many of the principles and concepts behind the writing of the successful 1978 book, **Money-love**, very little from that book will be repeated here, except when I take a point from that book and greatly expand on it. Or when I use a quote from what I like to call **Moneylove 1.0** to illustrate an important idea in **Moneylove 3.0**--as I do now by repeating the first sentence from the Introduction of the 1978 version:

*"You deserve to be rich, and you can be rich, **Moneylove** can help you have a life of abundance, filled with love and creativity and, incidentally, all the cash you want."*

Now notice that right up front even back then, I made it clear that prosperity consciousness is not just about accumulating or even earning lots of money. Love and creativity come first, and "all the cash you want," is just a side effect of true prosperity thinking.

Edwene Gaines

My friend and one of my favorite prosperity teachers, Unity minister Edwene Gaines, puts it a slightly different way, saying:

"Prosperity for me is a healthy body, prosperity is relationships that are joyous and satisfying and intimate and honest and nurturing, and that work all the time. Prosperity is work that we love so much that it's not work, it's play. And prosperity is all the money we can spend."

Not the Same Book, Not the Same Person

This is far from the book titled **Moneylove** that I wrote in 1978, which still has some solid and timeless perspectives on building prosperity consciousness and I am now far from the person I was in 1978.. (I now call that book, **Moneylove 1.0**.) We all live in a world that is far, far from the world we knew then. The changes have been dramatic and even traumatic, and your success in life (or lack of same) is largely due to how quick and nimble your reaction and adaptability and resilience have been during these sweeping changes. One of the changes that may have affected or concerned you on your path to a more prosperous life for you and your family is the widening disparity between the richest and poorest of us.

This is talked and written about a lot in this era of information overwhelm. However, chances are you are not at either of these extremes, but somewhere in the middle.

There is talk of the disappearing of the middle class. It hasn't gone anywhere, and in fact most of us are in it, certainly more people now exist between being really poor or really rich than did in 1978. But, as is often the case, all the talk, all the words expended in acknowledging and affirming the plight of the middle class, have only exacerbated the situation. Words are not actions, and little energy has been expended in dealing with the transformations that have taken place.

The changing workplace, changing economy, and changing world have often been blamed. The truth is there is more opportunity than catastrophe evident in all these changes. We've been caught up so intensely in the maelstrom of just trying to get by these changes, that we haven't taken the time to learn how to navigate them. As you'll soon discover, part of why I am more quick and nimble than many people, and certainly more so than most prosperity, motivational, and inspirational teachers, is that I was given time away from it all to study, reflect, meditate, and learn some profoundly new approaches to dealing with this changing world we live in.

In a very real sense, I was completely out of the workaday world, so I could think about what needed to be done and what needed to be taught once I was thrust back into action. I remember during my travails thinking, "This will either kill me or make me a much better teacher and writer."

A Conversation With My Readers

I want **Moneylove 3.0**, as was the 1978 book, to be like conversations I've had over the years with good friends who sometimes became my prosperity consciousness students, and in turn, even became my teachers and mentors. One was Louise Hay, whom I knew back in the days before she was a worldwide figure of inspiration. Louise more than repaid me for my prosperity coaching by saying when her book, "You Can Heal Your Life", came out and sold gazillions of copies, that "**Moneylove** is one of the best books on money."

Another was Jack Canfield, whom I first met in 1971 at a convention of The Association for Humanistic Psychology. I was a newsman for NBC Radio, covering the convention, and Jack was a bearded young workshop leader presenting a program called, *If Life Hands You a Lemon, Make Lemonade*. We became good friends and he and I co-led some Money and Self Esteem workshops. Jack was known as the expert on self-esteem, and I was being called "The Guru of Money."

One of the biggest laughs I ever got from an audience was from the prestigious Inside Edge leadership support group in Beverly Hills when I was introducing Jack and said, *"Jack has attended so many of my Moneylove seminars and I've attended so many of his self-esteem workshops that I now love myself a lot more than Jack loves himself, and he's a lot richer than I am."*

Book Ten:Laughing All The Way

If you see money and fun as two totally separate aspects of your life, chances are you won't ever have much fun making money.

Jerry Gillies

A sense of humor is part of the art of leadership, of getting along withpeople, of getting things done

Dwight D. Eisenhower

How many times have you laughed out loud in the past week? Your answer to this simple question can be an indicator of what kind of life you are leading.

The title of this chapter came from one of my favorite compliments ever paid to me. It was in a full page review of **Moneylove** by Og Mandino for SUCCESS magazine. He wrote,

"Jerry Gillies will have you laughing all the way to the bank. Gillies doesn't just lay down rules. He shows you with techniques that anyone can use, exactly how to accomplish all the objectives necessary to attract money–lots of it."

I recorded a tape way back in the 1980s called MoneyFun. It may not seem so now, but this was pretty daring then, as there was still a strong belief in the culture that money was no laughing or joking matter. In some segments of the population that is still true, but a lighter-hearted attitude about money and success is emerging.

During the Great Depression of the 1930s, some of the funniest comedy material in history was produced, in movies, humor magazines, and radio. A lot of the protagonists in the movies were rich, idle characters who had all the time in the world to enter funny situations, get romantically involved, or even solve crimes as in the exquisitely produced, written, and acted Thin Man series.

For over thirty years on radio and television, starting in 1933, Jack Benny was the most popular comedian in America. He created, during the Great Depression, his permanent persona of a penny-pinching miser with a manservant, Rochester, who complained about his stingy ways as an employer. A funny running gag on the show was when Jack visited his vault in the basement, usually chatting with a security guard who was also underpaid. It was a good counter to the doom and gloom throughout the land with massive unemployment and long lines at soup kitchens.

Benny's stingy, cheap character was so embedded in people's minds that many actually thought it was true, despite his being a generous philanthropist in real life. Other top comedians like Bob Hope, Fred Allen, and George Burns even made jokes about his cheap persona. One of the biggest laughs ever recorded in broadcasting history was when a mugger walked up to Jack on his radio show and said simply, "Your money or your life."

Maybe not a hilarious line, but you had to be there and know that everyone listening knew how stingy Jack Benny's character was, an image built up over years by the comedian and his great comedy writers. So when there was no response from Jack to the mugger's threat, the audience went into waves of belly laughs during the long pause that followed. With his always impeccable timing, before the first wave of laughter subsided, and after the mugger repeated his threat, "Look bud, I said your money or your life," Jack Benny brought the house down again with, "I'm thinking! I'm thinking!"

During the 2007-2008 economic meltdown, Jay Leno and other late night comedians had a field day with jokes about the economy, including Leno's running gag starting with, "The economy's so bad that "

There are actually three separate but very connected parts to the equation, and all are important qualities to have for full-blown prosperity consciousness to occur. There's a Sense of Humor, then Laughing, and finally Having Fun. If you can have or do all three when aspiring to improve your financial situation, your path will be a lot smoother and a lot more enjoyable. In terms of fun, Barbara Winter author of **Making a Living Without a Job** told me, "The way I run my business, when it stops being fun, I'm done."

Rev. Marla

Reverend Marla Sanderson, who also contributed to Book Seven, **Building a Prosperous Spirit**, is a longtime friend of mine going back to my Miami days in the 190s. She has founded The New Thought Global Network and easily met one of my major criteria for anyone I interviewed for this book: that they laugh at least three times during our conversation. Marla far exceeded that mark and always has had a vibrant and contagious laugh and sense of humor. She says:

Laughing is a purifying event, being able to laugh at yourself is an important part of having any self-confidence.

This idea of laughing all the way is one of the things my friend and business partner, Gregg, and I got out of all the Ken Keyes Jr. material we've studied and taught for so many years. When someone tells me something they think is going to offend me, usually it makes me laugh. I just find that I can now laugh at almost anything anymore.

And I need to laugh at pain. I do this in some painful physical therapy sessions. You get to a place where instead of screaming, you're laughing. People do find that strange. You can laugh a lot of stuff off.

https://spiritwithasmile.com/MS/

A Funny Thing Happened to Me on the Way to Parole

I certainly found all of what Marla says to be true during my twelve years in prison. It's an existence so weird and surreal as well as barbaric and dehumanizing, that you either laugh or go a little or a lot crazy.

Someone might say, "My work is so dreary and uninteresting that I cannot imagine seeing anything funny about it." Well, I suppose many people feel that way about prison, yet I laughed a lot, both out loud and inside my head during my twelve years of incarceration. It's often been said, "Humor is tragedy separated by time and distance. Maybe I didn't laugh so much in my first year behind bars, but I consistently lightened up thereafter, even earning spending money writing cartoon gags for several major magazine cartoonists.

I did do some prison gags, but also liked to weave something about the economy into the gag.

One of the ones that got me the most reaction from friends outside as well as fellow inmates, was the following bought by Bunny Hoest and John Reiner and appearing on the Laugh Parade page in *PARADE* magazine, the most widely circulated magazine in the world.

SCENE: One prison guard speaks to another as a middle-aged inmate stands in front of some cells with clothing and linen piled up in his arms.

CAPTION: "He says that, as a former CEO, he's entitled to a corner cell."

Another one that appeared in *PARADE* combined prison with the economy as well:

SCENE: One prison inmate on his bunk speaks to his cellmate.

CAPTION: "I took a year off to take stock of my life. Unfortunately it was other people's stock."

Many of the cartoon gags I did were about business, and one of the more successful cartoonists, Roy Delgado, sold a number of these to *The Wall Street Journal*, *Medical Economics*, *Barrons*, and the prestigious *Harvard Business Review*.

He also sold this full page color cartoon to *Readers' Digest*:

SCENE: One homeless man to another on a park bench.
CAPTION: "Actually, I couldn't care less what they do about the capital gains tax."

I wrote 10,000 gags during my incarceration on all sorts of subjects, including cats and dogs. I really missed my cat when I was in prison.

SCENE: Woman at desk with IN and OUT boxes on top of it. Cat sits in the OUT box, and she speaks to it.
CAPTION: "Yes, I get it."

I think that's enough of a sampling--don't get me started!
So I kept my sense of humor alive in prison, and even mined episodes from my twelve years there for parts of my one man shows when I got out. I also, as I've mentioned, plan to write a prison memoir. It's challenging, but I hope to make it funny, as well as uplifting and with a lot of lessons about overcoming adversity.

Someone I quote often and learned a lot from, the late Norman Cousins, was probably the first person who really understood the significance of humor and its impact on the brain and body. He said, "Laughter is inner jogging." He famously cured himself of a fatal illness by watching humorous videos such as the Marx Brothers movies, TV shows like I Love Lucy and Candid Camera, and teaching himself to laugh out loud.

Later of course, he led in the research that found out that laughter releases endorphins and other substances the brain secretes that have a major impact on healing and strengthening the immune system. His work, as first described in the bestselling Anatomy of An Illness, which was also an award-winning TV movie, is directly responsible for the fact that

Laughter Therapy is now used extensively in cancer clinics around the world. He is considered the godfather of the new science of psychoneuroimmunology. A lot of accomplishment triggered by a few good belly laughs. Norman said:

"Utilize laughter to create a mood in which the other positive emotions can be put to work for yourself and those around you."

I don't think it is too farfetched to suggest laughing a lot, seeing the humor in the absurdity all around us, and approaching one's work with a hearty sense of humor, will have a positive effect on one's cash flow.

Uncle Herb

I learned this from my Uncle Herb, who was a cosmetics company representative and had the job of going around to many, many drugstores (this was before they were called "pharmacies") in several Eastern states, and trying to get the manager or owner to either stock his products, or increase the order if they were current customers.. He always went in armed with at least one funny new joke. He made what was called, "a nice living."

I went around with Uncle Herb as a very young child of 9 or 10 on a few occasions, and the faces of the employees and/or the owner-manager would light up as soon as he walked in the door, because whatever else was going on, they knew that they would hear a great joke they could then tell at home or to customers. A number of top comedians learned their craft being salesmen, including one of the great joke tellers of all time, who became a huge star on TV and in Las Vegas, the late Myron Cohen, who was a salesman in the garment industry telling his jokes there for a number of years.

Seeing Funny Instead of Being Funny

Having a sense of humor doesn't mean someone is funny, is good at telling jokes or stories, can make people laugh out loud. That's great if it's a natural part of you. I saw that some aspiring young comedians at the San Francisco College of Comedy were just not that funny. They might have good stage presence and even good material, but they didn't have that instantaneous creative spark that allowed funny energy to be projected to an audience. They might, with lots of work, be able to make a living traveling the comedy club circuit, but unfortunately they're operating with a success ceiling in place and have no shot at becoming comedy super stars.

I once wrote some comedy for a young comedian in a similar situation. His father was very rich and powerful, and he was able to study with some top comedians. It produced results, even getting him some good TV exposure. But he didn't have what it takes to become a top-notch performer, he didn't have that almost indefinable something I call comedy charisma. If you watch old Johnny Carson TV clips of some of the major comedians of today, you will see that they might have been nervous and awkward, and maybe their material wasn't as funny as it now is, but they had something, and it was obvious. Look at old clips of Jay Leno, Robin Williams, Joan Rivers, and Jerry Seinfeld and you'll see what I mean.

I myself am not a good joke teller. I can get big laughs doing a standup routine with material that I wrote myself. But you can give me the funniest joke ever written by somebody else, and I just can't pull it off. So I learned to apply one of the great lessons we all hopefully learn in life: Put out the stuff you know you are good at, and keep anything else to yourself.

So what do I mean by seeing funny, and my view that it is sometimes better than being funny. I mean being someone who has a sense of humor and really can see the funny side of anything, even being in prison. It's like Marla Sanderson says, "I can now find I can laugh at just about anything anymore." That's what having a sense of humor is all about. And it is a lot easier to practice this and become someone that actually has it, than trying to be funny when you may not be. For me the term "sense of humor" is apt. It is like a sixth or seventh sense, giving one a new filter from which to view the world and one's life experiences. Seeing funny lets you laugh a lot at a lot of things and people are drawn to that cheerful energy.

The Jollytologist

My friend, author and speaker, Allen Klein, whom I first met at a National Speakers Association convention in the 1980s, is a prolific author of books on the power of humor, as well as books of great quotes. He has a fantastic sense of humor, and is delightful to be around. I still remember his childlike joy at finding out he finally had achieved a longtime dream, being invited to join the Macy's Thanksgiving Day Parade in costume, riding on a float.

Allen's first book, a bestseller, was The Healing Power of Humor. He travels the world speaking about the power of humor in all aspects of life, and is known far and wide as Mr. Jollytologist. It's another one of those serendipity things that's always happening in that almost at the same time I decided to title this chapter inspired by the Og Mandino compliment, I decided Allen had to be one of my primary interview subjects for both this chapter and QuoteLove. Then Allen told me a story I hadn't heard before:

You know, Og Mandino is the reason all eight of my quote collection books are still in print.

It was a presentation he did at the National Speakers Association. He said, "If you have a book proposal, come up after my talk. I will give you a label to send it to my publisher and he has said they will guarantee to look at whatever you send them within two weeks and get back to you." And that was very enticing to me because after publication of The Healing Power of Humor, I had a couple of hundred quotations left over that I thought would make a great book.

So I sent it to Og Mandino's publisher and they published my first quotation book, Quotations to Cheer You Up When the World is Getting You Down. When one publisher stopped publishing that book because they were cutting back, I got the rights back and sold it to another publisher, and there's been a demand for those books ever since, and it's all because Og Mandino gave me that label to his publisher.

If I needed to establish a connection between prosperity consciousness and a sense of humor, I wouldn't have to look too far. Allen Klein exemplifies both. He told me:

I have this very funny history with money When I was married, my wife taught me a lot about money. I wanted to save it and she wanted to spend it. Sort of like that line in Hello Dolly about money being like manure--you've got to spread it around and watch things grow. Nowadays, I find money almost every single day. Yesterday I was walking in downtown San Francisco and found a penny in one place, in another place, someone was on their cell phone and there was a penny right by their foot. They didn't even see it, so I picked it up. I always pick it up. At the end of the year, I divide my pile of found money by 365 so I can get a daily average. Some years it comes to 20 cents a day, sometimes 80 cents a day. It's amazing, and then I give all the change to charity.

Though Allen is a successful speaker and author, and lives very well, he still takes the time to enjoy discovering amounts of money that won't make a difference in his life. It's a fun project for him, and I might add that it adds to his prosperity consciousness by equating money with a fun game he gets to play every day.

Last month, I was walking down Haight street, and there was a hundred dollar bill on the street. My first thought was, "Oh, my God, the poor person who lost a hundred dollars." But then my second thought got me laughing, and I thought "Maybe it was a drug dealer, because there are lots of drug dealers on Haight Street, and if that's what happened, I don't care about that." I just started to chuckle.

I had a cousin who would say to me, "Allen, you're always finding money on the street. I never find money. Every time we go out you find money." Well, we were walking in the park one day, and I walked a bit ahead of her and dropped a dollar bill on the ground. Don't you know, she walked right over it! And I turned to her and said, "Look, there's a dollar bill." And she said, once again, "Oh, you're always finding money."

I think it's just a mindset, that I just believe now that money comes into my life. I have an affirmation on my wall I like, "I'm floating in piles of money."

And another affirmation I really like is, "The world treats me as royalty wherever I go."

So one of the things I came to realize and I also credit my wife for instilling this in me, is that money will come to you, so stop worrying about it, don't worry about money.

I've learned the lesson that if I am open to it, the money will flow into my life.

For over twenty years, I've been teaching people how to get more humor, get more fun, get more play into their lives. I certainly enjoy and love what I do, and bringing people more laughter and fun, and I have made money doing it.

In my workshops I want to give people an easy way to re- member to lighten up, so I use the word LAUGH.

L is for Let Go, because we can't get any laughter when we're over-upset or frustrated. One fun exercise I do for this is that I ask everyone to imagine whatever is stressing them out, and I give everyone in the audience a balloon and tell them to imagine they are blowing that stress into a balloon, and when I count to three, they release the balloon and see it as releasing that stress. So people see maybe 500 balloons floating around and they all start laughing. They might have to still deal with that stress, but it's a play- ful way, at least for a couple of minutes, of releasing and realizing that if they could do this for a minute or two, or even ten minutes, they start to let go of their stress.

The A in laugh is for Attitude, because I think as I said in a quote of mine that's gone viral,, "Attitude is like a box of crayons that colors your world."

Attitude is what you bring to the table every day, because you have a choice. If you're in a traffic jam, are you going to scream and carry on, or are you going to put on the radio and listen to great music, or think about your shopping list, or smile at the car next to you? It's your choice though. Every single moment, it's your choice in how you see the world.

I couldn't find a word I wanted that starts with U, so I cheat- ed and use Y.O.U., as in you've got to change your atti- tude, you've got to let go,

G is for Give. In my first book, The Healing Power of Hu- mor, I have fourteen techniques of how to increase your sense of humor.

One of them is really simple. As you know, Jerry, I love red clown noses. I have people in my audiences close their eyes and I pass around clown noses. They don't know what it is, but I have them think about some negative thing, and with their eyes still closed, I ask them to put this red clown nose on their nose, they still don't know what it is, and then they open up their eyes and look around the room and they start laughing. I ask them what happened to their stress, and they usually say it disappeared when they started to laugh.

H is for Humor, and to open your humor eyes and humor ears because there is humor all around.

As an example of this, I was in a laundromat and there was a sign on the wall that said: "WHEN THE MACHINE STOPS REMOVE ALL YOUR CLOTHING," which I did.

Allen told me this last one with a straight monotone but with such impeccable timing that I could see the scene he depicted in my imagination.

I asked him, "How about someone on their own, say a busy Internet entrepreneur, is there a good way for them to incorporate humor into their working day?"

Well I always have a fun toy or fun prop around. I look at it, i play with it, I have windup toys, and right now I'm looking at a Ronald McDonald puppet I have on my desk. I am looking now at an autographed copy from Woody Allen, my favorite comedian. I have a picture of my daughter with a cream pie thrown in her face, she wanted to have that happen. I can just look around the room and there are just fun things that if they don't make me laugh, at least make me smile, including a photo of me in the Macy's parade.

Someone might say, "Well, that doesn't change my stressful situation." Well, maybe not. Yes, you may still have to deal with that, but if you can get just a little chuckle, it takes your mind away from that stress just momentarily.

And if you chuckle or laugh, you get more oxygen in your brain, you're working better, you're thinking better. And it just takes you away from that stress so you can go back to it a little more refreshed

A little bit of humor or laughter is almost like getting up from your desk and walking around the room. It's a distraction, but it's a good distraction because it changes your focus. If you can get some laughter in anything, you get a different perspective. And you come back refreshed, and suddenly you may have a new idea because you're seeing something a little differently.

Moneylove Action Exercise

This reminded me of a fun exercise I often did in my workshops.

Take any amount of money you think will help you get the point that money is for fun as well as any other purpose. What I had my workshop participants do during their lunch break, was go to a store and buy something completely frivolous or even silly that served no useful purpose whatsoever other than as an object of fun. When they came back, we went around the group and each person held up their purchase and talked about how it felt to buy it.

You can accomplish the same thing either by visiting a store that has some frivolous things for sale, or going online to one of the many sites that features fun toys and playthings for sale. I have purchased many such items from www.thinkgeek. com, and a company that has special significance for me, www. ThingsYouNeverKnew.com.

A Childhood Pleasure

Things You Never Knew Existed does describe the kind of gags and practical jokes and novelties that the company has been selling for a hundred years, one of the oldest catalog companies in America. It actually started in Australia in 1905 when founder Alfred Johnson Smith started selling his fun items in Australia and it came to America in 1914 as the Johnson Smith Company.

Their catalog alone produced much joy for millions of kids, and I was one of them. It was 700 pages of silly, nonsensical, fun items, from Whoopee cushions to those little buzzers that gave your friends a shock when you shook hands, and many many more. I actually never bought that much from the catalog, but it still remains a fond memory.

To Laugh or Not Laugh With Children

I asked Allen Klein a question about an issue a lot of people let keep them from laughing more. "So do you ever get people worrying that if they laugh more and use more humor, they will be considered a lightweight or someone who doesn't take things seriously?"

Oh yes, one woman came up to me and said, "I can't laugh with my child. Because then my child wont take me seriously and I cannot discipline him. "I said to her, "On the contrary, if you can share some common humor with your child, it's a bonding thing." Victor Borge said, "Laughter is the shortest distance between two people."

If you're laughing about something you have in common, you're drawing closer together.

Studies have shown that if teachers could introduce four or five humorous things about the subject they're teaching, the students remembered it better and like the teacher more and do better on their tests.

That mother who felt she couldn't laugh with her child, I think she was totally off base, because the child may even listen more closely to what the mother says because they will enjoying being around her more.

Of course, if you are the boss, or even a worker, and you are laughing eight hours a day, maybe you aren't doing your job. So there's always this balance, of course. I don't think people should fear laughter, because I think it's such a great coping and communication and bonding tool.

As I said, Allen Klein is a great example of someone with prosperity consciousness, so I asked, "What about humor as a part of becoming more prosperous?"

Look at commercials. They use humor all the time to get their message across and get you to buy their products and increase their profits. So they're using humor to get more prosperity for their company.

I have noticed an amazing corollary to this, the fact that so many funny commercials are getting posted and reposted on social media, so that the companies involved are getting free advertising that would have otherwise cost them millions of dollars.

Humor is based on surprise, it takes you down one road,

and then... Someone once said, "It's like a train wreck of the mind." You're going in one direction and then totally go somewhere else, and so you start to laugh, because you feel duped, you feel silly, they 'got you' and you start to laugh.

Part of good joke telling is that you're surprised, you didn't think that was going to be the punchline. I sometimes tell a joke in my program about a woman who's in a nursing home. So after dinner, they're in a big meeting room and she raises her fist and says, "I will go to bed tonight with any man who can tell me what is in my fist."

A man across the room yells out, "An elephant!" And she says,

"You're right, you won!"

Even though I've been teaching humor for years, there's a wide spectrum. On one end are people who fear to use humor and on the other end, they may be using it too much. We all know people who will laugh at anything and it's hard to get them to be serious.

And there might be something underlying that behavior that they don't want to face. So that's not so great either. There's always got to be a balance of how you use humor, and where you use it. Are you using it to benefit yourself or other people, or you using it to put down and hurt other people?

To close a conversation I was enjoying a lot, I talked about something many people ask me when I discuss the importance of having a sense of humor as part of the way you present yourself to the world, "Do you think someone can be taught to have a sense of humor, when they've given no previous signs of having one?

Well, I think it all goes back to when we were children, and all children have this sort of innate sense of humor, you look at kids and they're laughing and playing a lot. And then it gets drummed out of them. You go to school and the teacher says, "Settle down, when are you going to get serious, Jerry?"

And your parents, you know, they're planning what college you're going to go to before you're in kindergarten. It gets so serious. But I think it's within us all. We all have a funny bone, but some people's funny bone is buried deeper than others because of the situation they grew up in and the people they grew up with. My dad didn't have a great sense of humor, but my mom was hysterical. And I think I follow my mom.

Allen's website is like a museum of comedy. He has some great articles, and great links to fun comedy sites, in addition to information on all his books.

www.AllenKlein.com

I have a confession here, as I was doing a final check for any typos or formatting glitches in Allen's comments, I had the thought that maybe I should have made Moneylove 3.0 funnier. I also, as often happens, had a funny line pop into my head, at least it seemed funny to me at the time: "If you become immensely wealthy, will you have to move because your poverty conscious neighbors will be saying, 'There goes the neighborhood!'"

Moneylove Action Exercise

This might be a good time to explore how deep your funny bone is buried. To look at your own history and early programming around humor and laughing out loud. Think about your parents and answer the following:

1. Did one or both of them laugh a lot?

2. Did they tell jokes? Or funny stories about things that happened in their lives?

3. Did they ever tell funny stories or anecdotes about the doings of other relatives?

4. At family gatherings when you were a child, did a lot of laughing go on?

5. Did they smile or laugh when you told them something you thought was very funny?

6. Did they ever tell you to stop laughing?

7. Did they threaten to separate you from a friend because the two of you laughed a lot when you got together?

8. Did they enjoy funny movies or comedy shows on television?

9. Can you name a favorite comedian of your father's? And one your mother really liked?

10. Who was your favorite comedian as a child and how do you feel about them now, do they still make you laugh?

11. Did you look forward to coming home and telling one or both of them about something funny that happened to you at school, or at play?

12. Did you do most of your childhood laughing at home or somewhere else?

My Funny Father

While Allen Klein thinks he got his from his mother, people who knew my father said I inherited his sense of humor. He was funny, but also often sarcastic, a trait I also have and try to moderate. I remember he would write jokes down on 3 x 5 cards so he could remember them, and since they were just shorthand cues of words to trigger his memory, I was frustrated that I couldn't decipher them.

My uncles and my dad's childhood friends all said he was a lot funnier than a boy who lived two doors down and became the famous comedian, Joey Bishop. When I was old enough to enter a nightclub, I would go with my father, and sometimes both parents, to see Joey perform during a run at Philadelphia's Latin Casino. Joey always made sure we had the best table, and I don't think my parents ever paid. We would go backstage to his dressing room, and Joey and Dad would tell stories of their youth on Jackson Street in South Philadelphia.

I was very aware at a young age that my father would have liked to have done what Joey did in the 1930s, go out on the road and tell jokes for a living. It was a big risk in those days of the Great Depression, and my father had a job and a wife, so he never went for it. He vicariously enjoyed Joey's many triumphs, always saying how hard he had worked for his success for so many years before being discovered and befriended by Frank Sinatra at an Atlantic City club. Joey was a member of the famous and notorious Rat Pack headed by Sinatra.

When I was preparing to start doing stand-up comedy, when I was enrolled at the San Francisco College of Comedy, I started a habit that continues to this day. I started watching stand-up comedy performances on my computer. Funny stuff is literally all over the Internet. I watched classic comics like Henny Youngman, Bob Hope, Jack Benny, Mort Sahl. I had even written some one-liners for Henny Youngman in the 1970s. Obviously, I have a sense of humor, and am easily able to think funny, but even if you've never had this quality in your life, you can definitely start to see things from a funny perspective by megadoses of comedy on a regular basis.

Leo Makes People Smile With Money

On the other end of that equation of Allen's finding money, there is Leo Quinn, one of my business partners who goes around in his neighborhood of upstate New York hiding new twenty dollar bills. He publishes clues on the website for people to find them, and the only stipulation he makes is that they use them at local businesses.

Leo told me:

I've always been a fan of giving away money. There's a guy who has a website called, www.GiveAwayaDollaraDay.com, and his idea is just to give away a dollar a day, hide a dollar bill somewhere, like dropping it in an elevator as he gets off when there's no one else around, so it may be found by the next person who walks on. I've done that with lottery tickets, and I like hiding one dollar scratchers around.

My favorite place to do that is in a bank drive-through. If there's a tube, I'll put a dollar scratcher in as I'm driving off. So the next person who drives up finds it. Maybe they win some money and that makes them happy. And they'll tell the people in the bank and others and it will have a nice ripple effect of happiness caused by a one dollar lottery ticket.

I've always been a fan of doing things like that. In late 2012 I saw an article online about a couple of guys in Boston who had been hiding twenty dollar bills every single day since September, 2011. So I thought that was a good idea and bought the domain name, www.findatwenty.com, and did absolutely nothing with it for a year. It came time to re-new the domain name, and it sounded like a fun idea.

The two guys in Boston had sort of turned it into a mar-keting agency, one of them was a lawyer, the other was a doctor. I already had a local marketing agency so I thought it would be a good way to get some notice for my business. In January, 2014, I hid my first twenty dollar bill here in my hometown of Ballston Spa, New York.

It was a snowy day, so I walked down to the post office and hid my twenty in an empty newspaper box in front of the post office. I came back, posted a clue on a Facebook page I had. Shortly thereafter, I got a call from the local newspa-per asking me what this new crazy thing I was doing was. And the reporter mentioned it on her Facebook page, and it was found very quickly after that. So it had a snowballing effect, and what I like about it is the person who finds the twenty is happy, their Facebook friends are happy, and I'm happy. There again is a ripple effect of happiness.

During my first year doing this, 2014, I had a couple of arti-cles in local newspapers, a TV station has interviewed me, and I'm up to almost 2800 fans on Facebook. Now every time I hide one it's found very quickly. Usually in under an hour, and sometimes under fifteen minutes from when I post the clue. So it's really been a nice way for me to get some notice about my own local business and to make a bunch of people happy. I think I've hidden almost 80 twenty dollar bills in the first year of doing this. Since I'm not com-mitted to doing it every day, I'm going to do it for as long as it's fun.

I have found that the more you give out, the more you get back. And I plan to keep testing that theory moving forward. I'm basically just a math teacher and in my local workshops, i just teach people the math of debt and how to get out of it the fastest possible way. So my workshops really have nothing to do with my hiding twenty dollar bills, they tend to focus on making small money moves to get out of debt faster.

More on Leo and what he offers at www.LeoQuinn.com

Secret Santa

There are a number of similar instances, and interestingly enough, all I've found have happened in the United States. Is it because it's the richest country of all, or is there some generosity of spirit in the American psyche that evokes this? In Kansas City, Missouri, for example, a wealthy businessman, who keeps himself anonymous by calling himself Secret Santa, has been giving away about one thousand hundred dollar bills to unsuspecting citizens every holiday season. In 2014, in early December, he moved beyond just giving them all away himself and enlisted the sheriff's department as deputy Secret Santas. What then occurred was quite amazing.

The deputies would stop a motorist, particularly one who looked like he or she could use the money, maybe it was an old model car, or had a dent in it. The siren would go on and the lights flashed as the deputy would pull over the motorist as if it was a routine traffic stop. You can imagine many of the drivers were not too happy at first, but immediately upon walking up to their car window, the deputy handed them a hundred dollar bill and said it was from Secret Santa.

There were shouts of surprise and joy, there were tears or looks of disbelief. And in the end, many of the recipients got out of their cars to give the deputy a big hug. Asked what he expected the police to get out of this new campaign, Secret Santa said simply, "Joy. The joy of giving."

You don't need to be a millionaire to feel the joy of giving. As one exercise I often suggested in my workshops illustrates.

Moneylove Action Exercise

You can do what I suggested my students do in the week following a Moneylove workshop. As long as it won't negatively impact your standard of living, get a new hundred dollar bill and just give it to someone you know, someone who doesn't need it, because it isn't to pay their bills or buy groceries. You say, "I'm giving this to you because it feels good for me to do it, and the way I am asking you to spend it is on pleasure. This may be a special meal you eat at a great restaurant, or it may be taking your significant other out for a treat, maybe a concert. As long as it is fun, and all I ask is that you let me know how much pleasure you got out of using it. You don't even have to tell me exactly what you bought, but just the feeling you got by anticipating and doing it."

Anything you can do to counter a lot of the negative images and thoughts around money will free up space in your consciousness to receive even more money into your life. Another exercise I did during workshops produced a lot of fun for everybody, and you can easily duplicate that experience:

Moneylove Action Exercise

This exercise I did a lot during lunch breaks, I had the workshop participants take $50 to $100 and go to a toy store. Their assignment was to buy something that looked like fun for themselves. Not for their kids or grandkids or nieces or nephew, but for them to play with and enjoy. This was challenging for a lot of the people, as you might find if you choose to do it. I suggest it will serve many purposes.

First, especially if you were not given free reign to get whatever toy you wanted as a child, it will give you a taste of splurging in a toy store. Also, it will tune you in to how the toy industry has changed since you were a child, and the different parts of your persona toys can appeal to. There are items of pure fun, there are things to tax your brain and help develop it, there are hobby items to build.

The idea is to pick something you haven't seen before, or haven't seen in years, and just buy it with the intention of playing by yourself and then deciding what other adult or adults you might enjoy sharing it with in a grown-up play date. As always, it will enhance the experience if you write about it, even very briefly, in your **Moneylove 3.0** journal.

Tony Busse

My friend, Tony Busse, who divides his time between New York and Panama, and is the person who intrigued and enticed me to move to the latter, is a good example of another part of the equation. The scheduling of play in the midst of work projects. In **TimeLove**, Martin Boroson and I talked about the smart new high-tech companies like Google, who are including a lot of recreation and playtime in the workday. Tony does this in his own entrepreneurial activities as well as including it when he trains small business owners on how to set up and succeed. He says:

My overall work philosophy has evolved into one in which recreation is a pretty important component. It may take a little bit of extra time, thought, and creativity to merge work and play, but I have found that in terms of my overall business, and actually my entire life, it's well worth the effort. It helps that today there a lot more opportunities available, a lot more flexibility in work and scheduling and so many more tools and technologies. For these reasons it's much easier to create that fusion of work and play. I don't even call it "work" anymore.

One of the things I'll do now if I'm starting a new company, is to have my being passionate about it as an absolute necessity in order for me to go forward. I only go forward with something that I get a lot of enjoyment out of doing. That's really the prime prerequisite before I go any further with an idea for a new business. Once I find something I think I will really love doing, I then start thinking creatively about how to make a business out of it, make money and interact with people by providing it as a product or service.

I really have evolved on this quite a bit. I started out as a very conservative business person, going by the book in terms of all the accepted formats of how to do business, back then there was a very big difference between business and fun. Over the years, I've lost a lot of the seriousness, a lot of the belief that there's going to be a lot of pain, struggle, or sacrifice involved in doing business.

Ironically, I found my results got a lot better when I relaxed got more comfortable and started having more fun. So now I regularly incorporate relaxation, recreation, and reward into my work day. I might have a piece of dark chocolate, or a meal I really like that I don't normally have for lunch or do some other pleasurable activity.

After accomplishing a certain task or milestone, which is usually a pleasant experience to start with, I will still give myself a little reward.

Tony is very good at flowing between his work and play modes. When he is in Panama very rarely do two weeks go by before he heads for the beautiful Pacific beach at Playa Blanca for a couple of days of rest and recreation. Tony is the author of a Kindle book called Go-Mode and the End of Mediocrity: Why Most Self-Help Material Hasn't Worked and How It Can.

Tony also developed the Go-Mode Tracker, a web-based app that people can use to track their progress in health and prosperity and every other aspect of a well-rounded successful life. More information on all of that good stuff at www.GoMode-Tracker.com

Go, Maggy, Go

Another friend of mine I interviewed for **Moneylove 3.0**, especially for Book Seven, **Building A Prosperous Spirit**, is Maggy Whitehouse, who's always in a go mode.

Maggy calls herself a Mystic for the Modern Age. She is a minister, and prolific author of such books as **From Credit Crunch to Pure Prosperity**, **Kabbalah Made Easy**, and **Prosperity Teachings of the Bible Made Easy**.

During our Skype chat for this book, Maggy told me she is taking a break from teaching prosperity to focus on the Kabbalah, and her newest career, stand-up comedy. We are definitely kindred spirits in many ways with many parallel paths we've taken. While I was an NBC newsman, she was a BBC reader (announcer). We have both spoken, talked, and written a lot about prosperity consciousness, and in 2012, we both decided to focus on writing and performing stand-up comedy. Though Maggy has been more disciplined, determined, and diligent at this than I have been--right now any comedy career I might have is on the back burner as I focus on this new book. Maggy is funny, and she has performed all over her native England. Maggy's comments on humor:

So much humor is nasty nowadays, and I think jolly humor is better for the serotonin. I think, in a funny kind of way, we have to surrender into laughter and surrender into spirit

and see how we can retrieve the prosperity in humor that isn't cruel.

I appeared as a comedian at the Edinburgh Free Fringe festival, and my audience was very different every night, but you could see that people were very open when you're funny about God. And open about feeling safe, and about the depth of spirit beyond religion and beyond the walls.

Maggy gets a big laugh from her comedy club audiences when she says she moved from being a minister to doing comedy because she was tired of performing for only five people every Sunday.

Of course humor is a very subjective thing, you might think something is hilarious while your friend or neighbor may find it lame. My own sense of humor is pretty eclectic, and like my friend Rev. Marla Sanderson, at different times, I can laugh at just about anything, including being in prison. I've used some Zen stories to illustrate some points in previous chapters, now in this one as well:

Have You Heard About the Zen Philosophy of Money?

You start with $50,000, Zen you have $12,000, Zen you have

$29.00!

"You will recognize your own path when you come upon it, because you will suddenly have all the energy and imagination you will ever need."

Jerry Gillies

Chapter Eleven: QuoteLove

I love creating quotes, sayings, aphorisms, and especially the way in which they often just pop into my conscious mind from some deep creative reservoir. I cannot tell you where or when I created the quote that is on the poster on the preceding page. I do know that it has had quite a strong life online. Originally in a poster created by WildWomanSisterhood.com, and more recently in this version created and posted online by The Master Shift organization, which I will talk about more in this chapter as they are among the most prolific distributors of uplifting quotes on their Facebook page. This one, within a day or two of its posting, got over 4000 shares and over 2000 likes.

I think quotes may have saved my life, or my sanity, or my career. When I was released from Folsom Prison in 2008 after 12 years of incarceration and no contact with the outside world, and never having been on the Internet, I was awestruck, literally could not take it all in at once, at how many of my quotes were being kept alive and well online. Friends on the outside had hinted at this in letters, one even sent me a page of my quotes from a website specializing in quotes. But I had no idea the extent of what I would find when I just Googled my name. Until then, broke and just out of prison, I had thought my teaching, speaking days were over, that no one remembered me and would not be likely to listen now that I was an ex-convict. The avalanche of my quotes told me otherwise.

Because quotes were so essential in my reemergence into the world, I started thinking about how we could get even more juice out of our favorite ones. Everyone seems to have favorites, myself included, and we read them, write them, post them on our walls or computer screen. But we don't do much to explore more ways in which our imagination can be applied to expand their impact on our consciousness.

This is why I created the very simple new process I call Quotercises. I am surprised no one came up with this before.

The core of this chapter is 100 exercises I have created to give you some new perspectives and perceptions about the quotes you enjoy and learn from. Some Quotercises are simple, some require a bit more thought and action. But all of them can teach you something new using a quote as your vehicle.

I've also included fifty of my own quotes, written over the past couple of years for my blog and Facebook, and for my audios. Plus fifty quotes from others, including many of my favorites, but also those suggested by many of my contributors to this book. The idea is to pick a quote that speaks out to you and then choose one of the Quotercises and try it out with that quote. I do caution you to not overdo it.

These are designed to be a permanent resource for your personal development and evolving prosperity consciousness, not a do-it-all-at-once process. You may want to explore a favorite quote with several of the Quotercises, but don't try to do them all at once or you will fry your brain, or at least slow it down in ways you may not appreciate.

I believe any single quote can make you happier and richer, depending on how you see and use it in your life--business and personal. I believe that the thousands of quotes we are bombarded with and surrounded by, thanks to the Internet, are a virtual treasure trove of tools for success and inspiration, perhaps the most under-utilized resource in any of our lives.

I have often found that when listeners to my audios or readers of my books, or even participants in my seminars come up to me and exclaim how something I demonstrated or said set them on a more sure path to prosperity--they repeat a specific sentence back to me as the fuse that set off the explosion into a new level of success.

What I find exciting is the fact that a quote from someone, even someone long gone, is a distillation of that person's entire life of learning and living and growing and thinking. The quotes we enjoy are actually touchstones of the ageless wisdom of the human experience. Author Nick Scheidies said, *"Quotes are a*

way to skip ahead and get years worth of wisdom in a single day."
I think the Quotercises make that even more true.

Here, for your consideration, are fifty of my own quotes:

1. There are many roads to success, but only one direction--forward.

2. At best, prosperity should be a side effect of living your true passion.

3. I think my ideal vocation is to be an oracle, to be consulted as the ancient ones were, but I'd live on the beach instead of in a cave and be very funny in dispensing my wisdom.

4. Money can buy you time but if you use that time to just make more money, whats the point?

5. Rich is about having a lot of money, wealth is about having a life.

6. People will respond much more readily to an invitation to go on a magnificent cruise with you rather than to helping you bail out a sinking boat.

7. There's no deadline on wisdom--good and inspiring ideas will not disappear--you don't have to hurry to grab them all right away.

8. Creating a heaven on Earth is the perfect prerequisite to reaching for the stars.

9. It's the person who understands time is worth more than money who produces the most money in the least time.

10. So when all is said and done, what have you said and what have you done?

11. The beliefs inside your head are not written in stone, but rather in neurons--which are definitely mutable.

12. Too many people are distracted by the search for gold out there and never find the diamond mine within.

13. Just as important as visualizing what you want is being awake enough to see it when it arrives.

14. When starting a new project is as exciting as starting a new romance, you are in the right career.

15. Do people smile when they think about you and what you are offering in the world? Then chances are you're successful.

16. There's nothing better than doing work you love in the place you want to do it, and no one telling you how to do it.

17. The more you prepare the ideal circumstances and environment to receive a windfall, the faster it comes.

18. It's not as easy to have a clear vision of what you want when people are blowing smoke in your face.

19. You should be as picky about the ideas you let into your head as you are about the people you let into your bedroom.

20. Making a dollar and making a difference do not have to be mutually exclusive.

21. The first step in successful harvesting of the Internet is knowing the difference between a healthy plant and a cow patty.

22. The more fun you have doing whatever work you do to support and enrich yourself, the more fun other people will have giving you money for the products, ideas, or services you produce.

23. If the world around you sucks, you may be fortunate in having the opportunity to discover the vast, powerful, fulfilling world within you.

24. In life, love, and the pursuit of happiness--one must always be aware that the occasional stumble is part of the process and makes the prize that much sweeter.

25. One of the most insidious poverty consciousness statements made: You can't have your cake and eat it, too. Of course you can--just order two pieces of cake!

26. It is impossible to waste time--it all moves you forward hour-by-hour, day-by-day, realization-by-realization.

27. The compliments you receive are powerful assets you can take to the bank.

28. Prosperity is about emotional satisfaction, not a pile of stuff.

29. When something you are working toward isn't working out, it's time to work deeper rather than harder.

30. If you have room in your heart, room in your home, room in your wallet--some amazing stuff may show up.

31. There is little that is as significant or as magnificent or as worth applause in this life as giving birth to a new idea.

32. If you're not as rich as you'd like to be, chances are you'd like to be richer than you really believe you ought to be.

33. When something you were working toward doesn't seem to be happening, it may be a time to relax and await the revelation of what you are meant to be working on instead.

34. Depending on other people to meet your needs can be a fool's game. Much better to expect the best from others, but leave attachment behind, and when they don't deliver on that expectation, just chalk it up to the fact you've had another encounter with an honest-to-goodness human being.

35. Even among decent, well-intentioned people, it remains rare to find someone who always says what they are going to do and then does it.

36. If you toot your own horn, don't act like you're the only instrument in the orchestra.

37. The best things in life are indeed free, but it is almost impossible to enjoy them if you are worrying about money.

38. The world is filled with people that can make your life easier, more prosperous, and a lot more fun--even if you haven't found each other yet.

39. The ultimate task is to keep in forward motion, always exploring new adventures, big and small--and always savoring the gifts life has to offer with gratitude, reverence and joy.

40. People can't rain on your parade if you don't tell them when and where you are marching.

41. Your success is guaranteed when you take a promise to yourself as seriously as one you make to someone you respect and love.

42. Optimists see negative events as minor setbacks they can easily overcome, and view positive events as evidence of further good things to come.

43. Money is the gravy of life--not the meat.

44. Some people don't need an inspirational or motivational book, video, or seminar. They need an inspirational, motivational slap upside the head.

45. Even when you are feeling down and insignificant, there are millions of people who would envy your life if they knew how great it really is.

46. The universe is loaded with money, you just have to find something worthwhile to exchange for it.

47. If nothing you do in the world scares you, or creates an uncomfortable or unpleasant feeling, you probably aren't reaching high enough, and are ordering short from life's menu.

48. If I told you the secret of success, wouldn't you be disappointed that there was no longer a secret of success?

49. Empty pockets come in handy when the universe is handing out large piles of money.

50. A shipload of money is ready to flow toward you if you've prepared an attractive enough dock.

And now to 50 quotes that have inspired, uplifted, entertained, or informed me and some of my contributors. To start with, we have ten quotes in a row from one of my favorite authors, who also happened to be a friend and mentor. I know of no one who was better at teaching creativity and writing, and who lived a fuller or more productive life.

Just reading his quotes you can get a sense of his childlike sense of wonder, and why he lived to be almost 92, submitting his last short story a few days before he died. Also, his quotes are worth exploring further with Quotercises. Try them.

Ten quotes by Ray Bradbury:

1) "You've got to jump off the cliff and build your wings on the way down."

2) "What's the use of being alive if you are not excited by life?"

3) "It doesn't matter what you do...so long as you change something from the way it was before you touched it into something that's like you after you take your hands away." Ray Bradbury in *Fahrenheit 451*

4) "If you stuff yourself full of poems, essays, plays, stories, novels, films, comic strips, magazines, music, you automatically explode every morning like Old Faithful."

5) "Everyone must leave something behind when he dies, my grandfather said. A child or a book or a painting or a house or a wall built or a pair of shoes made. Or a garden planted. Something your hand touched some way so your soul has somewhere to go when you die, and when people look at that tree or that flower you planted, you're there."

6) "I have two rules in life - to hell with it, whatever it is, and get your work done."

7) "Only the very young see life ahead and only the very old see life behind--the others between are so busy with life they see nothing."

8) "If we listened to our intellect we'd never have a love affair. We'd never have a friendship. We'd never go in business because we'd be cynical."

9) "We are cups, constantly and quietly being filled. The trick is, knowing how to tip ourselves over and let the beautiful stuff out."

10) As we come to my final Ray Bradbury quote, if you like what he says, there are a lot more online.

11) "Stuff your eyes with wonder, live as if you'd drop dead in ten seconds."

12) "You live but once; you might as well be amusing." Coco Chanel

13) A favorite of Barbara Winter's:

"A cheerful life is what the Muses love, A soaring spirit is their prime delight." William Wordsworth

14) Edwene Gaines' favorite quote:

"The purpose of human life is to serve, and to show compassion and the will to help others." Albert Schweitzer.

15) And one I like from Schweitzer.

"Success is not the key to happiness. Happiness is the key to success."

16) "Prosperity or lack of it is an outer expression of the ideas in your head." Louise L. Hay

17) "Sure sign of Spiritual Growth: You want more freedom, and less stuff." Lisa Villa Prosen

18) "Life lived for tomorrow will always be just a day away from being realized." Leo Buscaglia

19) "It's not what you don't have, it's what you do with what you have." Christine Segal

20)"There are three ingredients in the good life: learning, earning and yearning." Christopher Morley

21)A favorite of Rickie Moore's:

"No important life decisions are ever made consciously." Carl Jung

22) "We are all one planet--live with it." Rickie Moore, PhD

23) A favorite line from a favorite song of mine:

"Accentuate the Positive, Eliminate the Negative, and Don't Mess With Mister In Between." Lyrics by Johnny Mercer.

24) Sonya Milton, former minister at Unity SF. gave me this great quote: "The Inexhaustible Resource of Spirit is equal to every demand. There is no reality in lack. Abundance is here and now manifest." Charles Fillmore

25) And I like this longish but profound quote from Fillmore, founder of the Unity Church with his wife Myrtle:

"The mind is the seat of perception of the things we see, hear, and feel. It is through the mind that we see the beauties of the earth and sky, or music, of art, in fact, of everything. That silent shuttle of thought working in and out through cell and nerve weaves into one harmonious whole the myriad moods of mind, and we call it life." Charles Fillmore

26) "You have made spiritual progress when you can have your things or not, and be happy regardless." Edwene Gaines

27) "I have learned never to underestimate the capacity of the human mind and body." Norman Cousins

28) "A library is the delivery room for the birth of ideas, a place where history comes to life." Norman Cousins

29) "Nothing in the world can take the place of Persistence. Talent will not; nothing is more common than unsuccessful men with talent. Genius will not; unrewarded genius is almost a proverb. Education will not; the world is full of educated derelicts. Persistence and determination alone are omnipotent." President Calvin Coolidge

30) "Truly thoughts are things, and powerful things at that, when they are mixed with definiteness of purpose, persistence, and a burning desire for their translation into riches or other material objects." Napoleon Hill

31) "Applied Faith: the attitude that clears your mind of fear and directs it towards some worthwhile attainment." Napoleon Hill

32) "I am enough of an artist to draw freely upon my imagination. Imagination is more important than knowledge. Knowledge is limited. Imagination encircles the world." Albert Einstein

33) "Life is like riding a bicycle. To keep your balance, you must keep moving." Albert Einstein

34) I like this Christopher Morley quote --it may be my all-time favorite:

"There is only one success--to be able to spend your life in your own way."

35) And like Ray Bradbury, when I looked up Morley's other quotes, I liked them, too.

"Lots of times you have to pretend to join a parade in which you're not really interested in order to get where you're going." Christopher Morley

36) "From now until the end of time no one else will ever see life with my eyes, and I mean to make the best of my chance." Christopher Morley

37) "Read, every day, something no one else is reading. Think, every day, something no one else is thinking. Do, every day, something no one else would be silly enough to do. It is bad for the mind to continually be part of unanimity." Christopher Morley And Wow!

38) "Lighthouses don't go running all over an island looking for boats to save; they just stand there shining." Anne Lamott

39) More from one of my favorite writers of both fiction and nonfiction. "You can either practice being right or practice being kind." Anne Lamott

40) She does have a special quality of whimsey:

"You can safely assume you've created God in your own image when it turns out that God hates all the same people you do." Anne Lamott

41) "Now that all your worry has proved such an unlucrative business, why not find a better job." Hafiz, Persian Sufi mystic and poet.

42) "Every man is guilty of all the good he didn't do." Voltaire

43) Here is the favorite quote from Christine Segal of The Master Shift:

"Love does not consist in gazing at each other, but in looking outward together in the same direction." Antoine de Saint-Exupery

44) "The bad news is you're falling through the air, nothing to hang on to, no parachute. The good news is there's no ground." Buddhist teacher, Chogyam Trungpa

45) "The greatest thing in the world is to know how to belong to oneself." Montaigne

46) "Only a mediocre person is always at his best." W. Somerset Maugham

47) "There are very few human beings who receive the truth, complete and staggering, by instant illumination. Most of them acquire it fragment by fragment, on a small scale, by successive developments, cellularly, like a laborious mosaic." Anais Nin

48) "Man was born to be rich or inevitably to grow rich through the use of his faculties." Ralph Waldo Emerson

49) "You are always going to learn more by motion, momentum, and action." Internet marketing expert Yanik Silver

50) This quote expresses similar ideas to the one above, though written a few years earlier for sure:

"I know of no more encouraging fact than the unquestionable ability of man to elevate his life by conscious endeavor." Henry Thoreau

As a bonus, I'd like to include the following Emerson quote as it appears on a framed piece of calligraphy I found in a box and had saved from my Miami apartment wall in the 1970s

True Success by Ralph Waldo Emerson

To laugh often and love much
To win the respect of intelligent persons and the
affection of children
To win the approbation of honest critics
and endure the betrayal of false friends
To appreciate beauty
To find the best in others
To give one's self
To leave the world a little better, whether by a
healthy child,
a garden patch or a redeemed social condition
To have played and laughed with enthusiasm and
sung with exultation
To know even one life has breathed easier
because you have lived
This is to have succeeded.

Moneylove Action Exercise

So what can we learn from this 19th Century definition of success? One thing I learned was the definition of approbation, which I was a little vague about, it means appreciation, which some people substitute for the original word.

So one question I would ask as a check on my self aware-ness and path in life: "How many of these success markers have I collected? Another interesting question would be, "What one attri-bute of success would I add to Emerson's list?" Off the top of my head, I would add to the first item by saying, "And to be adored and thought the most important person in the world by at least one other person." And maybe, "To have all the time in the world to do with as I wish." And perhaps, "To do work that is so much fun that I sometimes feel guilty getting paid so much to do it."

There was a time when a provocative quote could set off lively and entertaining debate in a social setting or even with the debaters up on a stage with an audience. Maybe you might get some value out of starting a group like this among your friends or colleagues. I would think it could easily be as lively and worthwhile as a book club.

Jerry's First 100 Quotercises

And now, the Quotercises, to start to explore any of these or any other quote you choose with some new perspectives and new depth. The first step is always to pick or choose or find a quote from your personal favorites, or from the 100 just offered, or from a book like one of Allen Klein's quote collections, or from one of the many quote websites.

There really are two categories to Quotercises. Category One involves you choosing any quote at all and exploring it further with a Quotercise.

Category two are Quotercises that are sort of clues to a Quote Treasure Hunt, in that I suggest some criteria and you go out and find a quote that matches. It's pretty simple, and remember to enjoy the process!

1. Choose a quote and write a paragraph about what this quote means to you, and some episode in your life it may be describing.

2. Use your imagination to expand on a quote and how you might apply it to some situation in your life, or some lesson in your life it reminds you of.

3. Choose a quote and how does this quote seem to work in your life?

4. Decide to do something new for 24 hours based on a specific quote.

5. Explore applying the advice or idea in a quote to your life right now.

6. Choose a quote and imagine putting this quote on a teeshirt, and imagine someone coming up to you and asking you to explain the quote and why you are wearing it. Have a clear, succinct answer ready.

7. Pick a quote and write two short paragraphs about it. The first one is why you agree with its message, and how you might see yourself using it to inspire positive action in your life. The 2nd paragraph is what about it you might disagree with, or don't see applying in your life, or perhaps don't even understand the meaning of.

8. Think about this specific quote (whichever one you choose) in terms of how it relates to your personal money situation right now.

9. Choose a quote and memorize it, so you can repeat it to yourself throughout the day, and share it with some friends and/or colleagues to check out whether you all have similar reactions to the idea it expresses.

10. Connecting the dots. We often hear that term today, as a way of describing brilliance and success in someone--"She really knows how to connect the dots." In this case, I suggest you connect a few of the quotes, at least three, that seem relevant to some challenge or situation in your life. These quotes should fit well together in a synergistic manner, and also connect to whatever you want to get more clarity on in your life.

11. Imagine you have five minutes to choose a quote from any source and your life will immediately become a reflection of that quote in every area and aspect.

12. Pick a quote that you would be happy to have on your tombstone.

13. If your friends had to pick one quote to describe you and what you exemplify, pick one that most of them would agree with.

14. If you were filling out a profile for an online dating or match-making service and had to choose one quote that best describes your personal philosophy, which one would you choose?

15. Pick a quote that answers the question: What are your main aspirations in life?

16. Pick a quote that <u>least</u> describes who you are.

17. Pick a quote that if you saw it in calligraphy, framed on someone's wall, would immediately tell you that you found a kindred spirit.

18. Pick a quote and read it to yourself silently or out loud every night before you go to bed for the next thirty days.

19. Pick a quote that you think can be applied to successfully using the Internet even though it was written before the computer age.

20. Pick a quote that describes something you once believed but no longer do.

21. Choose a quote that means more to you now than when you first heard or read it.

22. Pick a quote you would use to give yourself or someone you loved comfort during a serious illness.

23. Pick a quote you would give to someone who has suffered a financial difficulty or setback.

24. Change a quote that is serious in a way that makes it funny.

25. Choose a quote from someone you know little or nothing about and find out more about who they were and what contributions they made.

26. Pick a quote that would annoy or sadden someone you know.

27. Pick a quote that had a major impact on your life and led you in a new direction.

28. Pick a quote that, if you wholeheartedly believed what it says and started living by its message, would make you a better and happier person.

29. Find a quote and rewrite it in your own words, in a way that keeps its philosophy intact but more reflects your individual character and desires.

30. Find a quote you wish every world political and religious and financial leader would read and start living by.

31. Take a quote and write your own that expresses the exact opposite point of view.

32. Pick a quote that, if they were doing a musical version of your life story, would make the good opening line of one of the songs

33. Find a quote that's new to you and to which you could respond, "That's exactly what I've always believed!"

34. Find a quote that perfectly describes your philosophy of life.

35. Find a quote that describes the way you respond to difficulty or obstacles.

36. Find a quote you realize you will have to think about and ponder before grasping exactly what it means and what its creator was trying to say.

37. Find a quote you like written by someone you have never seen another quote by, and Google their name with "quotes" following it, and find another one of their quotes you really like.

38. If you were asked to contribute a chapter to a book on being a more prosperous and lovable and creative human being, pick a quote you would want to be the opening of that chapter.

39. Make a list of Ten Quotes That Can Help Me Become More Successful, using five you've always liked, and five new ones you find in a book of collected quotes or at an online quote site.

40. Find a quote by someone you never suspected of saying something so wise.

41. Make a list of ten random quotes and write beside them whether you think they are uplifting, provocative, unclear, or profound.

42. Pick a quote that appealed to you but you never understood the full meaning of, and meditate on figuring it out.

43. Pick a quote by someone whose history you don't know and write a paragraph about what you think this person was like.

44. Pick a quote you wish your parents had lived by, and write at least a paragraph on why this is so.

45. Take a quote and rewrite it in a way that would make it more appealing to you.

46. Find a new quote that you would feel good about having with your signature on every email you send out.

47. Discover a quote you think illustrates that the writer was a much deeper thinker than you.

48. Find a quote that indicates the writer had more fun than you do.

49. Choose a quote that says to you that this person was a lot richer than you are.

50. Write ten quotes on individual slips or paper or 3x5 cards, shuffle them upside down, and ask a question about your current life you would really like the answer to, and pick one quote out and figure out why this is the true and perfect answer to your question.

51. Make a commitment that from now on, you will select one sentence from every book you read, fiction or nonfiction, that you find useful or inspiring.

52. Find a quote you wouldn't have appreciated or understood ten years ago, but find compelling and meaningful today.

53. Find a quote from a comedian from the past or present that makes you smile.

54. Choose a quote that you feel would make you change your life and your goals if you followed it exactly. Decide whether that would be a good or bad thing.

55. Look at a quote that has at least one verb, adjective, and noun, and pick a substitute verb, adjective, and noun and see what you come up with.

56. Pick a quote you wish you had said or written first.

57. Imagine you are asked to speak to an audience, and the person introducing you wants to say: (your name) the kind of person who epitomizes what (author of quote) meant when declaring that (pick a quote you would want them to use).

58. Pick a quote that describes someone you are no longer in a relationship with. Think about whether you would have gotten into that relationship if you were told this quote was accurately describing that person.

59. Find a quote that would have been a big help at a time in your life when you had a big decision to make. And write a paragraph about how it might have affected that decision.

60. Imagine you have spent a long, hard day, climbing a mountain to see a guru who lis sitting at the entrance to a cave at the top. When you reach him, he has a one sentence quote to give you that he says will make your life happier and more prosperous. Pick a quote that you would feel good about getting from this guru. Then pick another that would have you think about throwing him down the mountain. (sorry, the comedy writer in me couldn't resist).

61. Pick a quote you think your parents would have liked having on the wall of your childhood home.

62. Pick a quote you would have liked seeing on that wall.

63. Pick a quote that you think would inspire a bunch of sales people to go out and set new sales records.

64. If you were meeting a blind date, pick a quote that would make you feel better about the encounter if he or she were wearing it on a teeshirt.

65. Find a quote that reflects your opinion about dogs or cats.

66. Remember a favorite quote that made you smile or laugh when you first saw it.

67. Find a quote you don't like and would just as soon never come across again.

68. Find a quote that calls out to your heart and you would like to always remember.

69. Name three things that you like about a favorite quote.

70. Pick a quote you think would be good to tell a group of soldiers preparing to go into battle.

71. Pick a quote and decide what one word you use to describe this quote.

72. Pick a favorite quote that you promised yourself you would try to live by, but you haven't, and write a paragraph saying why this is so.

73. Find a favorite quote that no one knows is one of your favorites, and think about why you haven't shared this with people close to you. Pick a favorite quote that you promised yourself you would try to live by, but you haven't, and write a paragraph saying why this is so.

74. Find a quote you have never seen before that you would feel good sharing on Facebook.

75. Pick a quote you like and think about what it would be like to attend a party filled with people you don't know anything about, except that this was the favorite quote of all of them. Do you think you'd have a better time than you do at most parties you attend?

76. Find a favorite quote that no one knows is one of your favorites, and think about why you haven't shared this with people close to you.

77. Choose a quote that would make you feel more confident if you saw it on the desk or wall of a loan officer you were approaching for a loan.

78. Pick a quote you like and when you read this quote, do you feel it is something you exemplify in your life, or something you need to seriously work on?

79. Which quote do you think someone who knows you well would pick as likely to be one of your favorites.

80. Pick one quote and decide it will be your Quote of The Week. This means every day for the next week, you will devote at least 15 minutes to saying it out loud, or reading it, perhaps posting it on your computer desktop, or making a small sign containing the quote and putting it somewhere you can easily see it throughout the week.

81. Pick a quote you really like and find a brand new way of displaying it so that you get to see it at least once a day.

82. Find a quote you think is pretentious, one that sounds clever but really is confusing and doesn't say much.

83. Pick a quote that your friends would be surprised you like.

84. Pick a quote and imagine you and the person who wrote or said it were having dinner together. What would be the first thing you would ask them?

85. Pick a quote about one specific area of life, love, success, health, forgiveness, living life fully, friendship--and rewrite it so it refers to an entirely different part of life.

86. Pick a quote that mentions something you would really like to have and don't have now. Memorize the quote and repeat it over several times a day, but most of all when you wake up...and as you recite it out loud or in your head, picture yourself having and enjoying the item mentioned.

87. Choose a quote that you think would help a nervous friend about to be married.

88. Find a quote from a source other than this book that you feel represents the philosophy and psychology of **Moneylove 3.0**

89. Find a quote that contains the attitude you think best describes your view and perception of the world today.

90. Search for ten quotes you have never seen before, and when you have gathered them, think about the one that reaches out to you and your consciousness the most.

91. Pick a quote you feel epitomizes what you need to work on most in your life.

92. Pick a quote that describes the quality you think you possess that makes you attractive and interesting to other people.

93. Take a whole day off, in a very comfortable and pleasing environment, and go on a quote treasure hunt. See how many new quotes you can add to your personal collection that please you, inspire you, make you laugh, contain an important message for you, or provoke you into thinking in a new way about some aspect of your life.

94. Imagine you have been invited to give a college commencement address, and pick a quote you'd like to include in your talk.

95. Pick a quote you think would make someone, knowing you really like it, feel more favorably toward you.

96. Choose a quote that if you had it inscribed and put on the inside of your door, would feel good to read every time you left your home.

97. Choose a quote that, if you had it on the outside of your door, would make visitors feel good and perhaps feel they know you a bit better.

98. Go through this book and pick a quote by me or one of my contributors that you really like and feel you would get value out of paying more attention to.

99. Get in a very relaxed position, sitting or lying down, and just meditate for 15 or 30 minutes on one quote, and how your life might be different if you totally accepted and lived your life almost as if it were your personal motto. In this case, you might ask yourself

whether your life is nourishing, enthusing, and enlivening you--
then ask yourself whether you can see any connection between
your answer and how you view money in your life.

100. Choose a quote you like and think about how it might
apply to or describe some specific episode in your life.

Moneylove Action Exercise

Start to collect quotes as if you were going to do a small
book containing 100 hundred great quotes that people would enjoy reading, ones that haven't yet been widely circulated. You can
even create a few of your own, or invite friends to help you find
these. This can be a quick project, or you can take the next year
to work on it. At the end of that period, however long it takes, pub-
lish the book as a pdf book online, and start out by sending it to
everyone you care about, and then decide how you are going to
get it wider distribution Feel free to add any of my Quotercise you
think your readers would find useful. If you do this, you only have
to provide a link to www.MoneyloveBlog.com somewhere in your
book.

Allen Klein

I wouldn't feel I was doing this subject justice if I didn't ask
Allen Klein to share a few of his thoughts on quotes. He has a
number of collections of quotes in print, and one quote that he
wrote has gone viral on the Internet.

*"Your attitude is like a box of crayons that color
your world."*
As with many very popular quotes, there is more to it than
that single sentence. In full it goes:
*"Your attitude is like a box of crayons that color
your world.*

Constantly color your picture gray, and your picture will always be bleak. Try adding some bright colors to the picture by including humor, and your picture begins to lighten up."

Allen told me a funny thing that happens with this quote. It seems that there was a man with the same name spelled the same way, and because he was the manager of the Beatles and the Rolling Stones for a while, he is often given credit for the quote. The live Allen Klein (the other one died in 2009) sometimes writes to bloggers about the mistake they are making in attributing the quote to the other Allen Klein, but he often just smiles and shrugs it off.

Allen's thoughts on the subject of quotes and their sometimes interesting connections to each other.

At some point it's more than assembling quotes and putting them in a book. I notice that something Oprah said relates to something President Clinton said, and that relates to something someone else said. Suddenly they take on a life of their own and there's a flow to them.

Somehow a quote sings out to me, it calls out to me. And it's so easy today to find quotes on the Internet. Some I'm just drawn to, I identity with what they are saying, and maybe I'll feel its perfect at this moment for what I'm doing in my life.

A quote for me is kind of like an affirmation that i'm affirming either that this is happening, or I want this to happen. So it's something I want to see all the time. I believe the universe is full of energy, so a quote can help that energy come into my life.

I asked Allen if there is a specific length of time he keeps a specific quote as something to focus and meditate on.

I ask how does it move me, am I finished with this quote or not? When I find a quote that really inspires me, I keep it around a while.

But I also like keeping quotes alive by doing a quote cleaning every once in a while, perhaps once a month... removing any from my wall or computer folder that aren't reaching me at the same level any more. I may have gotten all I am going to get from them at this point. You can always go back and resuscitate them if you find your life would benefit from bringing them back into the foreground.

If I want something to happen, I might use the Goethe quote a couple of times a day, maybe when I'm walking the dog. I find that it helps me achieve what I want to achieve.

Allen usually uses a short version of the famous longer quote attributed to Wolfgang von Goethe, often called the German Shakespeare, who died in 1832 at the age of 82. But his authorship is disputed and this can be one way to play with some quotes that have some controversy or disagreement around them. I find it fun to research, usually using Google, what happened to and with a famous quote. I don't know if it really matters whether Goethe wrote it, or it was mistranslated from the original German, or actually written by a man named William Huchison Murray in 1951. It is still powerful stuff, and one of my favorites, too. In and of itself, it can provide enough material for an entire weekend workshop:

"Until one is committed, there is hesitancy, the chance to draw back. Concerning all acts of initiative (and creation), there is one elementary truth, the ignorance of which kills countless oneself, then Providence moves too. All sorts of things occur to help one that would never otherwise have occurred.

A whole stream of events issues from the decision, raising in one's favor all manner of unforeseen incidents and meetings and material assistance, which no man could have dreamed would have come his way.

Whatever you can do, or dream you can do, begin it. Boldness has genius, power, and magic in it. Begin it now." Goethe

This quote in its entirety, or in shorter excerpts, is worth repeating, a lot, for it is a powerful call to action, to doing it now. It definitely fits in with my clarion call to "Do the damn exercises!"

Moneylove Action Exercise

This is sort of a longer Quotercise, but I think appropriate for the quote I will continue to attribute to Goethe.

First, write or print it by hand on a card or sheet of paper, or even in your journal if you have one. Read it over every day for a week. And then memorize it. Say it out loud until you have it completely memorized word-for-word. Now you have created a tool that is accessible anytime you want a dose of inspiration. You can take if for a walk as Allen Klein likes to do. This is something worth letting into your mind attic.

A lot of people prefer just using the end of the quote:

"Whatever you can do, or dream you can do, begin it. Boldness has genius, power, and magic in it. Begin it now."

But I prefer focusing on the whole thing, as I think it sets our consciousness up for the strong finish. Some people feel the ending is a stronger, more direct, and more positive call to action. But I think that the earlier part contains a lesson about something we have all experienced, but often seem to forget. That once you decide to move forward and take those first action steps, the universe, or Providence, or whatever you want to call it, does seem to come in with unexpected and serendipitous assistance. Can you think of a time when this was true for you? In any event, you may be surprised at the impact memorizing the long version will have on your prosperity consciousness.

Barbara Winter

Some of the quotes I like most that have appeared on Facebook were posted by Barbara Winter who seems to have impeccable taste in great quotes and great blogs and websites she also shares. i download more stuff from her than any other of my Facebook friends.

I also owe her a debt of gratitude for inventing a term that perfectly describes many quotes, "Seminar in a sentence." I have adopted it.

I asked Barbara to share something about her experience with quotes:

> *I'm a voracious quote collector. And I've realized how often something I've memorized comes to the rescue when I'm feeling stuck or stumped.*
>
> *I think too many people don't pay enough attention when some of these wonderful thoughts come past them. But if we realize that even a tiny bit of information can get us back on track, or be the missing link in something that we're working on, it can have a profound effect.*
>
> *Five or six years ago, I was at my daughter's house and she got real serious and said, "I want to ask you something." And I immediate thought, "Oh, is this going to be about some family secret," so I said, "Okay, what?" And she said, "Do you have all those quotes in your head?" And I said, "I have some but not all of them in my head, but I do save them because I think they're really significant."*

Christine Segal

As Executive Director of The Master Shift, the nonprofit

organization that promotes worldwide synchronized meditations to work toward uplifting people and bring a shift toward peace, Christine Segal is a very active woman. She also, on The Master Shift Facebook page, oversees the creation of 7 posters a day featuring quotes from many sources, all positive, which are put out on Facebook to a very large fan base. The quote poster that opens **QuoteLove** was one of theirs, among several of my quotes they've selected. Quotes are obviously important to Christine, so I wanted to get her view on the subject:

I think quotes are very powerful and I think in particular before you go to bed, it's very, very, advantageous to read something positive, uplifting, affirming. This is so important because when you sleep, your subconscious is focused on the last thing that was in your conscious mind. If that last thing was an uplifting quote, it's penetrating deeper within you when you sleep. There's so many people who fall asleep with the news on--and they don't realize that all that negative stuff is just feeding into their subconscious minds. So, I always try to read something uplifting so that I go to bed with a smile on my face.

There's so many ways you can use quotes to uplift you during the day. If you can just read something that lifts you up and out of it.

Such a quote can really change you. And I think you have to really think about what that quote means to you and how you can interpret that into your life. With all the negativity around, uplifting quotes really lift people.

The person that creates the quote, their consciousness is in a high vibration when they do it. Quotes help us shift our mindset upward.

To check out the daily quote posters:
https://www.facebook.com/TheMasterShift

A Message Containing the Wisdom of The Ages

I know that many people take great quotes for granted. They'll see seven new ones each day on The Master Shift's Facebook page, or 500 in one of Allen Klein's quote books, and think they are just an unlimited commodity. But when we take the time to realize each one of those quotes came as a result of the writer's years of education, experience, and knowing, and that their consciousness, as Christine Segal says, "is in a high vibration when they do it," we get a larger sense of how magnificent each one is.

When you read a quote by an Einstein, or a Steve Jobs, or Louise Hay--or even someone you've never heard of, what you're experiencing is the essence of that person, their living legacy, a thought that may have taken a lifetime to build enough wisdom to create. If you pay more attention to a quote that calls out to you, you can touch some of the energy they had, some of the magic they shared with the world.

An Unexpected Source of Great Quotes

Many people overlook a great source of some powerful quotes. I have often mentioned my belief that anyone does themselves a disservice if they avoid reading fiction and only read nonfiction. As I quoted Maria Konnikova, the author of **Mastermind:** *How to Think Like Sherlock Holmes* in Book Three, The Law of Subtraction:

"Fiction writers are seeing a broader vista and are capable of providing you with insights or even ideas for studies."

This fact was a major part of my inner experience that got

me through prison. I've said that I read exactly 1000 books in prison, and a large majority of those were fiction, and most of those were mystery novels. Of course, I've already talked about the great quotes that meant so much to me in the Sherlock Holmes novels, but there wasn't a single mystery or other novel I read in which the author didn't have something wise or witty or compelling to say about the human condition. I kept the ones that intrigued or entertained or moved me the most in a school composition book, which I held onto and still treasure. Some of my favorite quotes from that collection:

"Wisdom lies in engaging the life you have been given as fully and courageously as possible and not letting go until you find the unknown blessing that is in everything." Rachel Naomi Remen

"Most of us come from the past and we recreate the present. Those who excel came from the future, their vision, their mission, and it pulls them forward." J. F. Freedman

"I think the happiness of a reader is beyond that of a writer, for a reader need feel no trouble, no anxiety: he is merely out for happiness and happiness, when you are a reader, is frequent." Jorge Luis Borges

"The man who doesn't read good books has no advantage over the man who can't read them." Mark Twain

"When you're young, you think everything you do is disposable. You move from now to now, crumpling time up in your hands, tossing it away. You're your own speeding car. You think you can get rid of things, and people too--leave them behind. You don't yet know about the habit they have of coming back. Time in dreams is frozen, you can never get away from where you've been." Margaret Atwood

"Prose should read like music plays in the heart." Eudora Welty

"We don't forget. Our heads may be small, but they are as full of memories as the sky may sometimes be full of swarming bees, thousands and thousands of memories,

of smells, of places, of little things that happened to us and which come back, unexpectedly to remind us who we are." Alexander McCall Smith

"The idea that the most strongly experienced moments--the particular moments were eternal. They actually went somewhere--into a file of moments that existed beyond time's range and could not be pilfered by God." Louise Erdrich

Book Twelve

Weapons of Mass Distraction

"Your heaviest artillery will be your will to live. Keep that big gun going."

Norman Cousins

I am not a big fan of military analogies, but feel my title is appropriate in this instance. As is Norman's quote. The more directed and diligent your attack on any residual poverty consciousness (which we all have) the better results you will see.

This short book contains seven exercises, strategies, or games that are designed to help you focus on some essential parts of your path to more satisfaction and prosperity in all areas of your life. From hearing about their experiences and results, some of those I have coached and given these weapons of mass distraction to have affirmed they can be powerful tools. Any one of them can make all the difference in the world toward achieving your aspirations and intentions.

Obviously, I believe in exercises and assignments and games and specific strategies. This is because I have seen them work, and because I seem to have an ability to create them. So much so that I have been paid to create experiential exercises to help a number of authors and self development teachers put their ideas into action in a workshop format.

The **Moneylove Action Exercises** and **Time Awareness Exercises** in TimeLove and my **100 Quotercises** in QuoteLove add up, I believe, to more action-taking processes than appear in any book ever written.

(You may have noticed I am not humble when it comes to telling truths.)

Whatever any of my contributors have offered as a way to remove or minimize that little negative Monkey Mind voice from your subconscious mind, I know from the response to my Drowning Stanley concept of losing that inner pauper voice in a sea of positive voices, that distraction works.

On the way to getting your negative inner voice under control, there are certainly times when you just want to push it to one side. Distraction is defined as something that takes your attention off something else. All seven of my exercises that follow have the potential to push you forward in some aspect of your evolutionary path to success and triumph.

Mass Distraction One

Your Anthem

I remember reading in the 1980s that one of the reasons Japanese workers were so motivated to produce, making their economy one of the fastest growing ones at the time, is that almost every company in Japan had a company song or anthem that workers sang when they started their work day.

Music is a powerful tool, and you may already have a selection of upbeat, positive songs you like listening to. Over thirty years ago i first became aware of the power of music to motivate and activate us in a workshop with Dr. Helen Bonny, pioneer music therapist and author of **Music and Consciousness**. Happily ever after that, I regularly

incorporated music into my prosperity workshops. One of my favorite songs since childhood is one I've mentioned a couple of times in earlier chapters. It's *Accentuate the Positive*, which almost sounds like a sermon. This is no accident because Johnny Mercer, who wrote the lyrics to Harold Arlen's music, got the original idea when hearing a sermon. I've said it's like an affirmation workshop all by itself. The great thing about writing a book in this 21st Century is that if I suggest a particular song, you can immediately Google it and hear it for yourself. If you are too young to remember this one, though there have been a lot of modern singers who have recorded it, check it out now.

Here's what I suggest, which you can feel free to modify as feels right for you. Pick a song that lifts your spirits and you think addresses your fondest dreams for the future. Make it your anthem, and listen to it at least once a day for thirty days to see how it works in your life. But to expand it's power, I suggest you learn the lyrics and sing along. If you are concerned about being embarrassed, find a place and time to be by yourself. You can gain momentum by doing a little dance as you sing to the song.

In addition to *Accentuate the Positive*, my personal song arsenal includes Zip-a-dee-doo-dah.

How can you resist lyrics like *"Zip-a-dee-doo-dah, zip-a-dee-ay. My, oh my, what a wonderful day. Plenty of sunshine headin' my way."*

I also like the song *Happy Days Are Here Again*, written in 1929 just in time to cheer up Americans during the Great Depression. It even became FDR's theme song. *"Your cares and troubles are gone, there'll be no more from now on, Let's sing a song of cheer again, Happy days are here again."*

Or newer songs like *Help is On The Way*, the lyrics of which were used to open Book Seven of this volume, **Building a Prosperous Spirit**, including, *"If you just hang in there, life is gonna work it out."* Google that one and prepare to be moved. Or Taylor Swift's *Shake It Off*, a favorite of Leo Quinn's. One coaching client chose The Stars and Stripes Forever march by John Phillip Sousa. He would march around his office or his home (usually when no one else was around) and pretend he was marching in a parade dedicated to his great success. Well, marches were designed to stir up the emotions. As Helen Bonny said, *"Music gives access to the discovery of inner strength, uncovers the potential for creativity, and manifests ways in which life can be lived from a center of inner security."*

So, if you're ready, pick your anthem and get going!

Mass Distraction Two
The Coin Toss

This could also be called "The Decider," though that might offend George W. Bush. It's a simple, childlike way to make decisions in your life that you have hesitated or avoided making. It has a catch to it which makes it a great psychological tool to help you know what you really want. It's a Weapon of Mass Distraction, because like all seven of of them, it requires your focused attention, thus taking your mind off any money worries or other difficulties you are facing. It originally came to me from a traveling troubadour who told me he loved the original **Moneylove** and it helped him decide to become an early Free Range Human, roaming the world, and playing his guitar and singing his songs in clubs and sometimes on the street. He wanted me to have the gift of his, as he termed it, magic technique for making quick and good decisions, such as what country he would go to next. As the name suggests, you just toss a coin and decide beforehand between two choices, which will be heads and which will be tails. Here's the twist: **You check in with your emotional response to the results of the coin toss.**

For instance, suppose you are trying to decide whether to take a trip to Panama or a trip to England. Say it's heads for Panama and tails for England. If tails comes up you check in with your emotions and see how you feel about that result. If you find yourself wishing it had been heads instead, just switch.

What this is really doing is allowing you a sort of psychological sneak peak at what your response would be once you actually make the decision. Most people find that they just can't imagine which would be the best decision, but tossing the coin and checking their internal reaction to the results has activated a preference they didn't know they had before.

You might try it out on some simple small decisions first, like which of two movies you would like to see at the mall. Or which of two desserts you will order.

The coin toss is a way to make more natural and rational decisions even though it may seem like child's play. The toss itself is exercising your decision-making muscle, and in a way that was impossible before deciding to toss the coin, you find out what you really want to do, as you know which result feels the best, and can reverse or correct it if you got the result that didn't feel right for you. It's really collaborating with your subconscious mind.

You can even toss a coin to decide whether you want to put one of these strategies into immediate practice.

Mass Distraction Three
Your Want List

This could be a big element in moving you forward. I first practiced this when I lived in a commune in a big luxurious house with 13 other people. Unlike a lot of communes in the past, most of these people were professionals who were gainfully employed. One of the practices they used to great effect was to have each resident prepare a Want List of ten items he or she really would like to have. They had to be possible to achieve, and the list was posted on each bedroom door. Come birthdays or holidays or anniversaries, everyone in the house knew what that particular person wanted.

I've adopted that concept in coaching sessions, with a major change. I ask that people ask for what they really want whether they think they have a chance of easily obtaining it or not. For what this mass distraction is aimed at getting people away from is "ordering short."

Even in very close, intimate relationships, partners often find it difficult, if not impossible, to tell the other what they really want, for fear that they don't deserve it, or will be turned down, or considered greedy. Whatever the reason, most of us order short a lot. Well, this Want List is for you and you alone. If you want a multimillionaire acquaintance to legally adopt you, write it down. If you want people to give you money to fund an idea you have, write it down. If you want that gorgeous person you would love to have a relationship with to reach out to you, write it down.

It's a secret list just for you, but it does awaken your subconscious mind to the things you weren't willing to ask for up to now. Does this mean you will get any or all of your requests fulfilled. No, but it does give you clarity about what you really want, and about what you might be doing to prevent your getting it. And the list can change and evolve. Every time you get something on the list, replace it with a new desire. And remember the spiritual lesson taught by Edwene Gaines and affirmed by the Catholic Archbishop of Chicago: every desire you have was put there by God, and you wouldn't have those desires if you weren't meant to get them fulfilled. Sit with that thought a while, and make your Want List.

Mass Distraction Four
Your Own Version

I called this **The Big Secret** in the opening Instruction Manual. You may well have figured this out on your own, but while you cannot edit or delete individual parts of a PDF file, you can highlight segments, copy them and then paste them onto a new page you create. Maybe you knew this, but digitally retarded me just discovered it. This is a tremendous opportunity and resource to really make **Moneylove 3.0** serve you well. Even if you were already someone who liked to go through and highlight passages or sentences in print books, this opens up many new possibilities. For instance, consider the following list of things you could do to more effectively take in the methods and messages that most appeal to you. If you read through the whole book before arriving at this last chapter, chances are a number of specific things struck a responding chord in you, tickled your fancy, or intrigued you in some way.

Now you can go back and copy just those parts that called out to you and basically focus on those. Here are three ways to do that.

1. Pick out one sentence or segment that really made a lot of sense to from each book or section, so that you knew you want to think about it more. Copy and paste it on your new document called **My Moneylove 3.0.**

2. Go through the books and focus on the interviews with my contributors, and again, in each interview, find one sentence or paragraph that appealed to you the most. Copy and paste it into your new **My Moneylove 3.0** document.

3. Finally, go through the book and pick out three action exercises you would be willing to commit to trying out in the next week. Again, copy and paste them into your **My Moneylove 3.0** document.

You now have a very abridged edition of this book that you created with your own choices. You can even print it out if you choose. Focus on this version for a full week, and see if it makes sense to have this option of building your own mini-**Moneylove 3.0**. If you chose, you could probably do this every week for some time. As you probably can see, it gets more parts of your creative mind involved in the whole effort.

Mass Distraction Five
Your Back Burner

I can only speak for myself and dozens of readers and coaching clients who have reported back to me how using this strategy worked for them. It was life-changing was the consensus, and that was certainly my experience. Of course, in Book Three, **The Law of Subtraction**, I talk about removing unused furniture from our mind attic. It's more down-to-earth than that when we talk about the Back Burner. When someone says, "That's on the back burner," we take it to mean that whatever that is isn't going to be acted on right now, it's temporarily deferred, moved to a lower priority, but with plans to reactivate it when the time is right.

This is what I suggest you do with every project other than the most important one in your life right now, the one that stirs up the most passion. Sometimes I suggest people use this in conjunction with the Ninety Day Trial Period I talk about in the **TimeLove** Appendix. When you have given something ninety days to bear fruit and it hasn't, you can have something on the back burner ready to devote your attention to.

What happened for me when I focused on my own individual back burner, where I could put all my aspirations and projects not ready for my attention yet, was I felt better about a bunch of delayed activities, because I knew they were waiting there on the back burner, and I was likely to get to at least some of them at some future date. And because I knew where they were and they were patiently waiting there, I did not have to give them another thought.

For instance, right now I know exactly what is on my back burner, it's not a vague pile of unfinished or never started projects. My comedy writing and performing is there, still simmering away. Since I have two new partners and have created this new book and a new Moneylove brand, I will be focused on that for some time to come. Every once in a while, I'll see or think of something funny and write it down and put it into my comedy file.

Also several book projects are sitting there, including my prison memoir. And two book projects with two different collaborators. I am excited about those, and they are definitely doing some enthusiastic bubbling, but remain on the back burner for now. For me and my clients, it seems to create a sense of calm about the stuff you really don't have the time for now. It's there on the back burner, and I am aware of the back burner's presence in my life.

The next step is for you to decide, if you don't know already, what your main focus is going to be for the next few months. We all know that you can only really pay attention to one major idea or project or passion at a time, otherwise you dilute your energy and attention and nothing wonderful happens. The back burner allows you to relax and do that. The step after you've know what your main activity is going to be, is to decide which other projects, ideas, activities you want to keep alive even though you won't be doing them now. It's important to know exactly what is on your back burner. Probably it's a good idea to use Dr. Maria Nemeth's formula and picture that you put those items on your back burner with clarity, focus, ease and grace.

The back burner strategy is a way of dealing with all the many opportunities now available to us, a way to focus on what is essential in our lives right now, and a way of maintaining distance, but not losing interest in some less essential items we may want to bring to the fore at some future time. For me, creating a back burner in my mind has changed the level of my creativity. You can do it any way that feels comfortable, but I actually picture a big shiny stove with a large burner in front for my current project and maybe half a dozen burners on the back row. If that isn't enough you can make your imaginary stovetop as big as you like.

Part of the whole back burner concept is about really paying attention to what is going on around you, and what is coming toward you, and what people are praising and acknowledging you for. If your current project, the one you are passionate about, isn't receiving any positive feedback, but one of the things on your back burner is, that might tell you something about your priorities.

Mass Distraction Six
Prosperity Partners

Like all these weapons of mass distraction, this one is designed to focus your attention on what is working in your life rather than what might not be working. The latest brain research shows that all the teachers and masters have been right that the mind can only effectively focus on one major thought at a time. The more ways you can have to assist in that focus, the more momentum you will create.

This strategy suggests you find other people to join you. Surely you have some friends or loved ones or even work colleagues who would benefit from this program, **Moneylove 3.0,** and enjoy sharing the experience with you. You might even share your self-created **My Moneylove 3.0** from Mass Distraction Four with them, or the **Moneylove 3.0 Triumph Document** from up-coming Mass Distraction Seven, if you prefer. Make them copies (you have my permission). One big advantage this provides is that you will get feedback of how you are doing. You will also get a sense of being accountable, especially about things like doing the damn exercises!

In your pair or group you can set some guidelines, but I would suggest that you agree that you will follow the formula to always say what you are going to do, in terms of material in this book, and then do it, and report to the other person or persons on a regular basis exactly what is going on, as they report back to you. Interpersonal support is a valuable tool in any learning ex-perience. You can do this in person, or if your prosperity partner is in another city or even another country, bring Skype calls into your prosperity program. You set the boundaries and rules, but if you agree, I think once a week would be a reasonable time to schedule meetings or calls.

Mass Distraction Seven
Your Triumphant Moneylove 3.0!

At some point after first reading the book, you will have in-stituted some of the suggestions and strategies into your life. This may seem a pretty ambitious distraction, but remember my pur-pose is to have you move forward in terms of fun and knowledge and increased income. If you did even a few of the exercises and even only focused on one or two of the 12 Books, you probably have begun noticing some positive results. This is a way to ac-knowledge and reinforce those gains.

The task, should you choose to accept it, is to go back to the beginning of **Moneylove 3.0** and go through the entire book, with your highlight, copy, and paste fingers ready. Pick out those passages and suggestions and **Moneylove Action Exercises**, or **Time Awareness Exercises**, or **Quotercises** that you feel added to your success, and copy and paste them in a new **Moneylove 3.0 Triumph Document.**

This is similar but different to distraction number four in that instead of a short abridged version of the book you designed for yourself to study from, you are creating a full volume showing what has brought you to this level of success in your endeavors to expand your prosperity consciousness.

You can also start off this new document by listing ten things you think you've gotten so far out of this whole experience, since you first received **Moneylove 3.0** and opened it on your computer. Remember one of the goals as emphasized in **TimeLove**, is to own your time, so you can do this final Weapon of Mass Distraction whenever it feels right. That may be a few days or a month or even a year after beginning. Whatever works for you. And this should be one of your mottos in this adventure. As David Friedman said during our interview when we talked about all the different approaches being offered in the book, including his Thought Exchange technique, "Whatever works, go for it!"

One good final question to ask, at least up to this point, is whether you think and feel you are better off today than you were on the day before buying **Moneylove 3.0**? I welcome your feedback and any success stories you would like to share.

Editor's Note:

We hope you've enjoyed the Third and Final Volume of Moneylove 3.0 and that you've gotten great results from the various exercises listed within it. It has been a true pleasure assembling and making available this final product of Jerry's that was so close to his heart. Jerry put a lot of Fun Effort into creating Moneylove 3.0 and was very eager to share it with as many people as possible.

We are very honored to have played a small part in helping him accomplish those wishes and truly hope you enjoy and get value out of each of the 3 Volumes. We join Jerry in wishing you a life that is filled with a steady stream of "Joyful and Triumphant" experiences.

Additional Resources:

We are very pleased to continue Jerry's policy of always giving people more than their money's worth, as such we've got two great offers for you.

By using the link below you will receive a Free Audio of Part 1 of Jerry's iconic Money Love Audio series

http://www.gomodetracker.com/moneylovefreeoffer

In Addition...

The same link will also contain the following exclusive offer related to the Go-Mode Success Tracker mentioned several times in Moneylove 3.0:

A FREE Copy of the book "Go-Mode the End of Mediocrity" as well as close to 50% off of the amazing Go-Mode Success Tracker accountability tool.